ESSENCE

ESSENCE

The Diamond Approach
to Inner Realization

A.H. ALMAAS

Samuel Weiser, Inc.
York Beach, Maine

First published in 1986 by
Samuel Weiser, Inc.
Box 612
York Beach, ME 03910

Reprinted, 1988

ISBN 0-87728-627-2
Library of Congress Catalog Card No. 84-51109

Typeset in 10 point Baskerville
Printed in the United States of America

CONTENTS

Dedicated to the Three:
The Sage, The Mage, and The Seer

PREFACE

AS HAS BEEN WRITTEN A THOUSAND times, the ultimate
nature of essential reality cannot be communicated in words. However, this reality manifests in pure essential forms of consciousness
and experience, in what we call the "aspects" of essence, such as love,
strength, peace, compassion, awareness—to name only a few. The
experience of these aspects is completely palpable and subject to
keen and precise discrimination. It is this fact that allows the verbal
descriptions and analyses that this book undertakes.

The concept of essence is found in some spiritual traditions,
such as Sufism and some schools of Buddhism, though the word
"essence" is not always used. In more common usage, "essence"
means that aspect of something most true, real, or substantial. It is
the essence of something that makes it what it is. In the course of this
book, our usage will become increasingly clear, and in fact we will
ultimately see that the "spiritual" and "common" understanding
converge in a deeper, more subtle and yet simpler way than it is at
first possible to appreciate.

Beginning to understand essence means beginning to see
through our illusions. This book describes the way many things are
mistaken for essence in spiritual and psychological work. This book
also describes the loss of essential qualities, and the subsequent
separation from true being, that occurs during individual ego
development—thus shedding light on the whole story of personal
suffering that has sprung out of the illusory reality of the individual

ego identity. The lives of most people involve a constant effort to "prop up," defend, promote and improve this identity, whose status as a mental construct is never challenged. Thus the liberation and joy of knowing our true identity is lost, unless the desire for a deeper or truer experience of being is allowed to manifest, and we have an opportunity to search effectively for the truth about ourselves.

This book introduces a method for the retrieval and development of essence, so that it can function as a transformative agent in the process of self-realization. In the course of this movement toward realization, the stabilized manifestation of the qualities of essence leads to a surprising and unusual resolution of an age-old dichotomy, an unexpected redemption of the personal life: the realization of the "pearl beyond price," described in Chapter Five, constitutes a resolution of the apparent conflict between the life of the "man of the world" and that of the "man of the spirit."

CHAPTER ONE

PRESENCE AND ESSENCE

N GENERAL, PEOPLE RARELY have, and never recognize as such, the experience of essence. So we will begin by looking at a related quality of experience that is more commonly felt and talked about: the quality of *presence*. The expression "I am present" is often used in spiritual and psychological circles, with an assumption that its meaning is understood. We ask: what *does* this expression mean? What does being present actually signify? Most of the time the expression is not used in a very definite or clear way; most people, if asked, are unable to explain what they mean by "present."

But there must be an actual condition that warrants using the expression "I am present." What is that condition? The expression literally means that there is an "I" that is present at the time. Is this literal meaning accurate?

Obviously, when we say "I am present," we don't mean exactly that we are aware, otherwise we would say so. There is a difference between the meaning of "I am present" and the meaning of "I am aware," although the two can and frequently do coincide. What is the difference? What makes us say "present" instead of "aware?" What is in the experience of "I am present" that is different from the experience of "I am aware?" What is the element that accounts for presence?

We want to inquire into the meaning of presence by contemplating and analyzing the actual experience of presence. Let us examine a familiar situation, the aesthetic experience. My eyes catch the sight of a beautiful red rose. Suddenly, my sight is clearer, my smelling is keener. I seem to be *in* my seeing, I seem to be *in* my smelling. There is more of me here, seeing, smelling, and appreciating the rose.

This phenomenon is not simply one of increased awareness, so that more of the rose is experienced through my eyes and nostrils, so that more of the rose is experienced through my perceptual system.

In the experience of increased presence, it is as if I meet my perceptions midway. It is as if something of me, something more or less palpable, is present in my eyes and in my nose. Something in me besides my perceptual channels is participating in the experience of the rose. And this something is not memory, not past associations with roses.

In a sense, my greater awareness actually enhances the presence of the rose, or of any aesthetic object, such as a piece of music or a painting. Sometimes greater awareness enhances only a certain quality of an object—the beauty of the rose, its color, its smell, or its freshness. But sometimes the rose as a rose, as a presence in itself, is felt. If that experience is deep enough, our own presence is enhanced. "I seem to be more here," the expression goes. But what is this presence? Is there really an "I" that is more present, or what exactly is it?

Of course, the aesthetic experience is not restricted to a response to beauty alone. It might be the experience of awe when confronted by the immensity of the ocean or the grandeur of a mountain range. It can be the experience of admiration when one witnesses heroism in an individual or a group, or the courage or boldness of an explorer.

We are considering the moments, however rare they are, when we feel as if there is somehow more of us partaking of the experience. We want to understand what "more of us" means. More of what? What is the element that gives our experience this taste of presence?

We are also aware that some individuals have greater presence than others. We say, "He has more presence," or "He's an imposing presence." But can we say what is really being referred to here? We are not referring to the quality of presence of mind, which is greater awareness. "Presence" itself is more than that.

Presence also can be sensed at times of intense and deep emotion, when a person is fully feeling an emotional state, not controlling or inhibiting it, when he is involved wholeheartedly in the feeling, totally immersed in it in a free and spontaneous way without judgment or holding back. This usually happens only when the person feels totally justified in feeling the emotions.

For example, an individual might experience a great loss, like the death of a loved one, and so feels justified in feeling the grief and the sadness. He might get so involved in the sadness, so immersed in it, that the feeling deepens as if it were miles deep, going to greater depths and profundity. This state might become so deep and profound that it feels thicker and denser as he gets more deeply immersed in it, so deep and profound that he experiences himself permeated by a kind of presence. It is as if the profundity and the depth *are* an actual presence, palpable and quite clearly there.

Another example: A person might feel justified in feeling angry and indignant about being insulted or unjustly treated. The anger becomes so powerful that at some point, if he goes goes unreservedly with the feeling, the person will experience in the anger some kind of force powering it. This force or power is so clearly manifest that it assumes a palpable presence. It is as if the mounting power of the unrestricted emotion evokes more of the person. He feels himself so present in the emotion, so at its center, that a clearly sensed and substantial presence seems to infuse the emotion and fill the body. His body feels packed with power, so densely that power becomes a presence. This presence seems to be the source of the emotion and power, both in it and behind or under it. At such times, the person experiences intense contact with the body, along with an astonishing capacity to use and direct it. It is as if at that moment the individual actually exists in his arms, for instance, and hence can use them with an unusual amount of control, efficiency, and immediacy.

Now, what *is* this presence that exists in the arms, in the body, that seems to bring with it power, energy, contact, and awareness? We are seeing that presence is more of an actuality than an idea or a metaphor. We are getting a sense that presence is much more profound, more real than feeling or emotion. We are approaching, although still vaguely, an appreciation of what presence is.

The presence one experiences does not have to be one's own, and does not have to be individual. One can experience the presence of another. A whole group can be aware of a presence. Even one who is not particularly attuned to the quality of presence cannot but contact presence is some unusual and unique circumstances. One such situation is that of a mother giving birth to a baby.

At times, when the mother is not under medication, when she is fully participating in the birth, her presence may be elicited. The mother may feel a fullness, a strength, a solid determination, an unmistakable sense that she is present in the experience, fully involved in it.

The situation of giving birth is real; it is not social, and it cannot be faked. For a woman to do it in full consciousness, without the aid of mind-dulling medications, she might have to pull out all of her resources, pool all of her strength and determination, and be genuinely present.

This full presence of the woman also may be sensed by others. One may see it as the presence of intensity, of intense feeling and sensation, or of intense energy and attention. One also may be aware that the woman is present in a way unusual for her. She seems to have a fullness. She seems to have a glow, a radiance. The presence is unmistakable, beautiful and powerful.

The experience of presence in this situation may be seen, if one is sensitive and aware, not to reside only in the mother. If all present are fully participating—and this often happens in such situations because of their dramatic intensity—then the presence is seen to pervade the room, to fill it and impregnate it. There is an intensity in the room, a palpable aliveness, the sense of a living presence.

The experience of presence is most clearly felt when the baby is born, when it is out into the world. One may then experience a shift, an expansion in the energy of the room. One feels that the room definitely has a new presence, a fresh presence. The baby is experienced not only as a body but something much more, something much more alive and much more profound. One may, if sensitively attentive, behold the newcomer as a clear and definite presence. The baby is a being. A being is present, with no name, no history, no extras. And there is blessing.

One may in fact observe that different babies have different qualities of presence. The quality of presence is not just a matter of their size, how they look, or what sex they are. Each seems to have its own unique quality of presence, which is quite obvious at birth and which continues to be the mode of being for the particular baby. One may behold the emerging presence of the baby as a sweetness, a fluffiness, a tenderness. Or the presence is felt as a peacefulness, a quietness, a stillness. Yet another baby confronts us with a presence of clarity, lightness, and joy. Another might fill the room with strength, solidity, and immovability.

This experience of a situation being filled with a certain presence also may be felt in the purity and aloneness of nature. In moments of quietness and solitude in nature, a person becomes aware that the natural environment itself has a presence that profoundly affects his mind and heart. It is not uncommon, when one is not occupied with the concerns of the world, when the mind is empty and still, that nature presents itself not only as the objects constituting it but as a living presence.

A range of high, rocky mountains can then be felt as an immensity, a solidity, an immovability, that is alive, that is there. This immensity and immovability seems sometimes to confront us, to affect us, not as an inanimate object but as a clear and pure presence. It seems to contact us, to touch us. And if we are open and sensitive, we may participate in this immensity. We may then feel ourselves as one with the immensity, the immovability, the vastness.

Just as mountains have their particular presence, so do forests, oceans, rivers, and meadows. One may even sense the presence of a tree, as Krishnamurti relates in one of his solitary contemplations:

"There was an intensity about the tree—not the terrible intensity of reaching, of succeeding, but the intensity of being complete, simple, alone and yet part of the earth. The colours of the leaves, of the few flowers, of the dark trunk, were intensified a thousandfold. . . ."[1]

We can expand our inquiry by considering presence in situations of stress or danger. Sometimes, a person under extraordinary duress, when his ability to function might be expected to be reduced, will be saved by a surprising power or capacity surging from within.

---

[1] J. Krishnamurti, *Commentaries on Living*, 3d ser., ed. D. Rajagopal (Wheaton, IL: Theosophical Publishing House, 1977), 80. With the permission of the K & R Foundation, Ojai, CA.

His perception will suddenly become acute, his mind lucid, his body agile and responsive. He will experience a level of courage and intelligence not normally available to him, an extraordinary strength and will, an unusual command over his mind, emotions, and movements.

At such a time, great feats can be accomplished in response to vital needs. A person might feel, dimly or lucidly, that a power has awakened in him. It is as if the whole being has gathered in one integrated intensity, which makes possible the emergence of a calm strength, a poignant presence that deliberately and knowingly acts according to the needs of such a moment. Excitement is gone, emotions are absent, and thoughts are stilled. What remains is exactly what is needed to meet the emergency.

What matters for our discussion of presence is that in those rare crises of life and death, when our ordinary capacities for perception and action fail us, there can emerge in us a power hitherto unknown: a calm and collected presence that can take charge and act unhampered by our thoughts and emotional states. This condition is not experienced simply as the absence of hampering thoughts and emotional conflicts. There is, rather, a positive presence of a power, of a superior intelligence that is not physical, emotional, or mental.

This potential increase of presence in dangerous situations is utilized by some people, adventurous or athletic types, in the form of seeking or arranging situations that make it necessary for them to be intensely present. We are not speaking of the person who looks for emotional excitement by getting involved in dangerous situations, but rather of the individual who, knowingly or unknowingly, seeks situations of danger where excitement and emotionality are an impediment, where instead, calm strength and intelligent presence are required.

This potential of situations of extraordinary duress is recognized and utilized by some systems of self-development. The disciple is encouraged to stay awake and present in situations of extreme emotional difficulty or physical fatigue. At such times the usual everyday mind cannot function. The individual will tend to discharge emotionally or go to sleep if the fatigue is the result of prolonged lack of sleep. But if he is kept awake, and willingly attempts to be present in this situation, there might emerge within him an intelligence or a strength that would change his whole situation.

In Zen Buddhism, this is accomplished by giving the disciple a koan, an enigmatic phrase or question that cannot be understood by the discursive mind. The person goes over it in all ways possible for him, mentally and emotionally, until he reaches mental and emotional exhaustion. If he is ready, and if the situation is ripe, then a momentary silence and stillness in him will bring a flash of *satori*, an emotionless and wordless realization. Inexperienced followers usually assume that the realization must be some kind of insight. However, the deeper realizations in Zen are glimpses of beingness, of being-as-such, of the presence of reality. The deep realization is the experience of presence.

G. I. Gurdjieff, the Russian teacher, used the method of subjecting students to extreme duress. He frequently put his disciples into situations so difficult that most of them believed they would be impossible to tolerate. The students might walk long distances for days, beyond their ordinary endurance level, or they might perform menial tasks for days without sleep.

Some thought that the purpose of these efforts was to build a certain kind of strength and endurance, which is partially true. The real significance of those situations emerges when we understand that at the same time the students are supposed to practice "self-remembering." Self-remembering is defined here as paying attention to both inner and outer environments. Some of his students assert that self-remembering also means maintaining the awareness that one is paying attention.

In fact, this practice is only an exercise that will lead in time to actual self-remembering, which cannot be explained to a person who has never experienced it. If Gurdjieff had meant by self-remembering splitting the attention in two—one part directed inward and one part directed outward—he would have just said: pay attention inside and outside. Why bring in the word *self* and the word *remembering*?

One might argue that self means what we experience inside, plus our awareness or attention. This would include our emotions, sensations, and thoughts, plus our awareness of them, but this perspective is limited. It is due to not knowing that our inner experience doesn't actually include other categories of experience.

We see the Gurdjieffian practice of self-remembering as the first step, the initial effort needed for real self-remembering to happen. However, if we limit ourselves to this understanding, we might never recognize the experience of true self-remembering because our preconceptions will function as barriers to our experience.

Gurdjieff insisted that usual efforts are useless for self-development. He talked about super-efforts, efforts that transcend the usual limits of the personality and are not directed toward satisfying its usual small needs. "Man must understand," he said, "that ordinary efforts do not count. Only super-efforts count. And so it is always and in everything. Those who do not wish to make super-efforts had better give up everything and take care of their health."[2] Super-effort "means an effort beyond the effort that's necessary to achieve a given purpose," said Gurdjieff.

> Imagine that I have been walking all day and am very tired. The weather is bad, it's raining and cold. In the evening I arrive home. I have walked, perhaps twenty-five miles. In the house there is supper; it's warm and pleasant. But, instead of sitting down to supper, I go out into the rain again and decide to walk another two miles along the road and then return home. This would be a super-effort. While I was going home it was simply an effort and this does not count. I was on my way home, the cold, hunger, the rain— all this made me walk. In the other case I walk because I myself decide to do so. This kind of super-effort becomes still more difficult when I do not decide upon it myself but obey a teacher who at an unexpected moment required from me to make fresh efforts when I have decided the efforts for the day are over.[3]

Of course, such super-efforts will develop strength and will, but Gurdjieff is more interested in self-remembering than in strengthening a person's capacity to endure. Certainly, part of the purpose lies in developing this capacity, but it is not the main purpose. An individual needs only to join the army to learn endurance; he doesn't need to work with Gurdjieff.

---

[2] P. D. Ouspensky, *In Search of the Miraculous* (New York: Harcourt, Brace & World, 1949), 232. Used by permission.

[3] P. D. Ouspensky, *In Search of the Miraculous*, 347. Used by permission.

Gurdjieff's method is to cause a friction between the consciousness of the individual and his habitual manifestations, so that in time, and under the right circumstances, there will emerge in him a taste of self-remembering. In writing about considering how to accomplish certain tasks that he set for himself, he describes how the totality of his mentations lead, at some point, to the conviction of the possibility of attaining all of his tasks as a result of the forces arising from the friction of his consciousness with the automatic manifestations. He describes how at the end of this perception "my whole being was filled as if by some singular, never till now experienced feeling of joy.... Simultaneously with this, in and of itself, and without any manipulation on my part, there appeared the sensation of so to say 'self-remembering,' also of a never-before-experienced vigor."[4]

It is obvious that here Gurdjieff refers to self-remembering as a sensation and not as an activity or an insight. But we ask, sensation of what? He says it is the sensation of self-remembering. But we are attempting to understand what self-remembering means. At this point we understand only that self-remembering is a sensation of something.

Our understanding here is that this sensation is nothing else but the sensation of presence. It is the awareness of presence in oneself. Gurdjieff's methods were designed to help the person be so present in those situations of stress that presence becomes a palpable, definite experience. Anyone who has an impression of Gurdjieff, through personal experience or though his writings and work, will undoubtedly experience Gurdjieff as a presence. We can call it power, we can call it will, or we can call it strength. Nonetheless, the impression is very definitely of an impressive and powerful presence. This is a presence that confronts us. It is a presence that is beyond the words and the specific actions, a presence that is Gurdjieff.

And Gurdjieff's presence is Gurdjieff. That is why he uses the term *self*. It is he who is present as an actual palpable presence, beyond his words, ideas, and actions. So we can say that what is meant by self-remembering is just that. It is the remembering of self.

---

[4] G. I. Gurdjieff, *Life Is Real Only Then, When "I Am,"* 3d ser. of *All and Everything* (privately printed by E. P. Dutton for Triangle Editions, 1975), 42.

Gurdjieff meant the phrase literally and simply. People who don't understand make this sound quite complicated, but when self-remembering happens, it is seen to be literal and simple; what is real in the person is present, remembered after being forgotten. Gurd-jieff's called his last book *Life Is Real Only Then, When "I Am."* There is reality only when I remember myself, when I experience that "I am." He also asserts in the same book that a person can do—that is, act consciously, intentionally, and without conditioning—only if he is present, if he exists consciously.

Here we remember those situations of extraordinary duress where an individual can act unhampered by the usual ordinary states of consciousness. So, according to Gurdjieff, these situations involve states of self-remembering. What we called presence is here seen as the presence of what is real in a person. "I am present" means "What is real in me is here." It is the conscious experience of existence. It is the experience of "I am."

Although we have made the connection between presence, self-remembering, and the experience of "I am," a person might object that it is very vague and nothing has been proved so far. This is true. We are not trying to prove anything. This is not a logical argument. We are only seeking an appreciation, a taste, for a realm of experience that the mind cannot grasp directly. It is a realm that cannot be reached by logic and argument. It can only be ex-perienced directly, and that is why there are schools and systems devoted just to engendering and developing this experience.

In discussing Gurdjieff's usage of the concept of self-remembering, we have been able to connect the experience of pres-ence and the experience of existence. "I am present" is the conscious experience of "I exist." It is the awareness of a living presence existing, being. It is not simply the awareness of the many thoughts, feelings, and emotions, which awareness is the preliminary require-ment for self-remembering, and not self-remembering as yet.

Gurdjieff called the real part of us, the part that can experience "I am," our essence. He defined essence as the part of us we are born with and that is not a product of our upbringing or education.

So in the experience of presence, what is present is essence, our true nature, which is independent of conditioning. Presence and essence are the same. We have discussed presence to give a taste of what essence is. As we see, essence is the part of us that is the experience of "I am." Essence is the direct experience of existence. Of course, essence can be experienced as other things, such as love, truth, peace, and the like. But the sense of existence is its most basic characteristic. It is the clearest, most definitive aspect that sets it apart from other categories of experience. Essence *is*, and that is what is most basic to its experience.

This experience of "I am," of direct apprehension of existence, is not a mental or emotional experience and cannot be understood from the perspective of the usual categories of experience. The mind can think about existence, but it cannot reach it. We have seen this in discussing presence. The answer to the question: "What is essence?" is "what is in us that can experience 'I am.'" Essence is the only thing in us that is directly aware of its own existence. Awareness of its existence is an intrinsic quality of essence. A Tibetan author puts it, "Hence (experientially) a founding stratum or existentiality (sku), and a founded pristine cognitiveness (ye-shes), having been such from the very beginning that the one cannot be added or subtracted from the other, are present like the very nature of the sun (and its light)."[5]

One might argue that all people know that they exist, although they might not know their essence. This is both true and false. They know that they exist, but they do not know it directly. The usual knowledge of existence is through inference; it is not a direct knowledge. This point has been discussed extensively by philosophers. The usual mode of knowledge of existence is epitomized by Descartes' *Cogito ergo sum* ("I think, therefore I exist"). We can infer existence only from various kinds of experience. Usually, we think that we exist because we can see our bodies, hear our voices, feel our sensations, and so on. Descartes was more refined in saying that we know we exist because we know that we think.

So there is always an inference from some perception. And the inference is of something that we are very vague about. When somebody says, "I think, therefore I exist," what does this person mean by "I"? Is he clear about what he means?

And because there is inference, there is no total certainty. There might be logical certainty. There might be commonsense

---

[5] Longcchenpa, *Kindly Bent to Ease Us*; pt. 3: *Wonderment* (Emeryville, CA: Dharma Publishing, 1976), 7.

certainty. But there is no real, deeply felt, existential certainty. The certainty doesn't exist in inference because experiential existential certainty needs direct experience, in fact, the most direct perception and experience.

The most direct perception and experience is the one of identity, when we are what we experience, when the perception is so direct that what perceives and what is perceived are the same thing. This is exactly the experience of essence.

Here there is no inference from something else. It is the most direct experience. The experiencer and the experienced are the same thing. There is no separation between subject and object. The subject and the object are the same: essence.

It is not only that there is no inference. There is also no intermediate medium for the perception. Usually there is an intermediate medium that enables a subject to experience an object. When the eye sees an object, the intermediate medium is light, but when essence is aware of itself, there is no intermediary. The object, the subject, and the medium of perception are all the same: essence. Also, the organ of perception is essence itself. There is in the experience only essence. Essence is the subject. Essence is the object. Essence is the medium of perception. Essence is the organ of perception. Essence is the experience. There is no separation whatsoever, no duality and no differentiation.

The experience of essence as existence, the experience of "I am," is not as if there is a subject that is the actor of existence. The "I" and the "am" are not separate. The "I am" is a unitary experience. The nature of the essence, of the real self, is existence. The "I" itself is existence.

So it is more accurate to say that the part of me that is existence is present. Essence is the only part of me that actually exists, in the sense of experiencing itself as pure existence, pure presence.

We have investigated the question of presence, and we have seen that presence is the presence of our essence. It is the real part in us, the part not conditioned or produced by the environment. It is our intrinsic nature. We have seen that essence is the only part that is aware of its own existence directly, intimately, and with certainty.

Essence is not simply the only part of us that is aware of its existence. It is what exists. It is not only what exists, but it is also existence. This existence is not only the nature of man but the nature of everything. It is the unity of all, or as Shabistari, the fourteenth-century Sufi, puts it:

> There is one atom greater than the whole—
> Existence; for behold the universe
> Is, yet that universe itself is being.
> Being is various in outward form,
> But in its being bears inward unity.[6]

In experiential terms, presence and existence are somewhat different but only in degree. Presence is the presence of essence, of that which is existence. However, we must go very deep into this experience of presence to experience the most basic nature of essence, which is existence. So presence is the presence of essence. Existence is the inmost nature of essence, which sets it apart from all other categories of experience. When this experience occurs, it is not vague, unclear, or undefined; it is not an intuition or a fleeting insight. It is a very definite, clear, precise experience of "I am." There is definiteness and there is certainty.

---

[6] Mahmud Shabistari, *The Secret Garden* (London: Octagon Press, 1969), 71.

CHAPTER TWO

ESSENCE

N THE FIRST CHAPTER we approached essence by considering presence, for a fundamental reason: most of the time essence is not recognized when it is present. This is because people generally restrict their attention to the usual, normally accepted categories of experience, and essence does not fall within those usual categories of thought, emotion, and physical sensation. Hence, it is always missed, even by the interested individual. The person does not conceive of a different perspective. Even if he allows himself the idea that there is such a reality, he does not know where or how to look.

The difficulty is that the reality that is sought is in a form that is not expected. The person might even be looking it in the face but not realize it is what he is looking for.

There is a Middle Eastern joke that illustrates this point: Nasrudin has become a smuggler. He is seen crossing the border with his donkeys laden with goods. The customs officials search everything but never find anything of value, although they know that Nasrudin is a successful smuggler. The officials allow him through each time, exasperated that they cannot spot the contraband. But it happens that the officials are staring right at the thing they are looking for: Nasrudin has been smuggling donkeys.

At other times, the difficulty is that it does not occur to the individual to look in certain directions because he is accustomed—conditioned—to look only in familiar directions. This is similar to the individual who does not know that he can experience energy directly in his body. Whenever he feels any inner movement in his body, he believes it must be the movement of his blood, or that there is something physically wrong with him that requires medical attention. So when there is a strong energetic discharge as in a deep emotion, he never knows that he is perceiving energy itself in its movement.

This example of energy is a good one because it also brings out another factor in the mystery. The movement of energy is felt directly in the body usually when the movement is large. Small movements are not usually perceived by most people. However, by training one's sensitivity one can learn to be aware even of subtler movements.

This is also true when it comes to essence. There is a need for deepening and refining one's perceptivity. However, even when this happens, essence might not be recognized because one does not know that there is such a thing; or one might confuse it with something else, like confusing energy with the circulation of blood.

Our true nature, essence, is like the donkeys or like energy in the analogies above. People who don't recognize essence usually imagine it as a mysterious reality or force. But it is mysterious only to those who don't recognize it. For the one who knows, it is a very clear and definite presence, just like the presence of the donkeys. For such an individual, it is not even a subtle presence. It is subtle only for those whose attention is customarily attracted and caught by the usual kinds of experience—thoughts, emotions, and sensations—or physical movement within the body. The mind in its customary condition is crowded by all kinds of contents that are gross in comparison to essence. When the mind is emptied of its usual content, we can see that essence is as clear and as definite a presence as a bright star on a clear dark night.

The person who has realized essence does not experience it once in a while, as a special unique occurrence. This pattern is the usual one for the ordinary person under the best circumstances, but it is so for the realized person only at the beginning. In time, essence becomes a permanent and abiding presence, and the person progressively identifies with it as his true nature and identity. It becomes the ordinary experience of the individual every minute of his life. The fullness of essence is then permanently present and is the center and the source of the individual's life and actions.

Having discussed essence in terms of presence, we need to say more about what it is not and contrast it with other categories of experience, so that we more fully and accurately understand essence as presence.

Essence and the Mind

Essence is not a thought or an idea a person has about himself. It is not self-image. In fact, the self-image, the collection of concepts one has of oneself, is one of the main barriers to the recognition and development of essence. The self-image usually does not include essence, so essence becomes habitually excluded from one's experience. Even a person in whom essence is flowing may not experience essence if the self-image excludes it, just as a person might manifest anger only unconsciously if the self-image excludes angry behavior.

A concept, a thought, or an idea might arise out of the experience of essence, might be generated under the influence of essence. This sometimes happens in expansive ideas of discovery and revelation. But the thought is not essence. The influence of essence on mind is most obvious in certain kinds of poetry written when the poet gets a taste of essence—when the words, thoughts, ideas, and images are generated by essence and attempt to reflect and communicate the essential experience. Very often the poet is not directly aware of essence but is aware only of the idea, the image, and perhaps the emotion produced by the contact with essence. The poet may become so enamored of his words and images that he never moves to the actual direct experience of essence. The words can be beautiful and the images enchanting, but all this beauty and enchantment fall short of the beauty and enchantment of the essence itself.

Poetry becomes more real when the poet is directly aware of the presence of essence. Then the words and images more closely reflect the truth and are less distorted by the personality of the poet. We call this kind of poetry objective poetry, which is a phenomenological description of the poet's experience of essence. This is the most beautiful, most inspiring, and most powerful poetry. Images that simply describe essence surpass in beauty the imagination of any poet, for essence is the source, the power, and the stuff of poetry. But even the most accurate and powerful description of essence is not, we must remember, essence itself.

There is a certain class of images that people customarily see or take as essence; here we are referring to visions. Such experiences happen to some individuals especially at intense emotional times. When the experiences are frequent, the individual is called a visionary. The person might see visions of Christ, Mary, saints, angels, paradise, and hell—all kinds of scenes and happenings—usually in vivid colors, accompanied by intense emotions. These experiences are usually thought of as spiritual. They are spiritual if we define spirituality as having visions, but certainly they are not the same as the direct experience of essence. Essence is something much more fundamental, much more real, and much more substantial than visions. If the person is content with or even enamored of his visions, then he might never recognize his essence, his true nature.

There is very often a connection between essence and vision, but usually the connection is concealed from the visionary. However, if this connection is seen and understood, then the person can use the vision to contact essence directly. What happens is that the individual experiences a taste of essence but is not directly aware of it. His contact with essence touches him in a deep way and produces deep emotions, which are translated in the mind into religious symbols and images. In some cases the images come first, and seeing the images provokes deep religious emotions. The individual is usually aware only of the images and emotions. But these are simply reverberations in the mind of the contact with essence. The relation of visions to the essential experience is like the relation of dreams to the reality they express. The dreams are distorted and symbolic images of processes that the dreamer is not directly aware of.

Obviously, if the person focuses his attention on the images and emotions of a vision, he will miss entirely the true underlying reality, the presence of essence. The visionary experiences will seem unique and special and will not be used to deepen understanding. Often the person feels blessed, and the people around him consider him to be spiritual.

The individual actually is blessed, but he is blessed by the contact with essence, not by the vision. In fact, the vision, as we have seen, can be a barrier, a veil over the real essential experience. The vision is not an objective perception. It is very much formed and colored by the particular person's history and present mentality. This is why Christians have Christian visions, Jews have Jewish visions, Hindus have Hindu visions, Buddhists have Buddhist visions, and so on. These experiences, although they might be called religious or spiritual, are not yet the perception and the experience of our true nature, our essence, the truth that is in us.

Many teachers and many of the true work traditions actually differentiate between spiritual experience and the experience of essence, the true reality. The Sufis, for instance, assert that there are three forms of knowledge: intellectual knowledge, spiritual knowledge (which they see as more emotional in nature) and the knowledge of reality.

The second form of knowledge, the spiritual knowledge, is the knowledge of states, psychic powers, occultism, and the like. However, the true knowledge of reality is much more basic and much simpler than that. It is the direct perception of being, our nature. And it is not emotional or intellectual.

Visions fall within the second category of knowledge. They are not yet the true experience of reality. Here we understand how the psychologist Carl Jung fell short of understanding essence. He got closer to the experience by his formulation of the archetypal images, but images, as we see, are not the essence. He saw essence, in all of its archetypes, as images that came clearest in visions and dream images. His own experience was from images in dreams and visions in his waking hours. In fact, all of his archetypes are images of certain essential states but are not the essential states. He saw the self, for instance, as a very deep archetypal image that gives us certain deep experiences and impels us toward certain actions. But in reality, the image itself is a production of essence, or more accurately, the response of the mentality of a particular person to the presence of the essential experience of self. A person might have deep emotional feelings about the archetypal image of self, but this is not the same as experiencing the essential self.

Jung also had the image of the wise old man, seen as the guide for inner transformation. This image is a reflection of a certain essential aspect that functions as guidance but also has many other functions not expressed by the image of the wise old man. Other images, in other systems, that are related to this essential aspect include the following: the guardian angel, the angel of revelation, the holy spirit, the angel Gabriel, the witness in heaven, the body of knowledge, and many others. Such images depend on the individual's mind and are not exact reflections of the essential aspect. This particular essential aspect is a certain presence, very definite, very clear, very precise, very palpable. Gurdjieff called it "objective consciousness," and the Taoists called it the "diamond body." One who directly contacts this essential presence can understand easily what particular facet of this presence each archetypal image refers to.

We see that Jung got very close to essence and its various manifestations but stayed on the level of imagination because of his mental and visionary bent of personality. So he fell short of realizing his essence and living it, and his psychology remained a mental construct not directly connected with the presence of essence. He did the same with alchemy, using its images and ignoring the substance of its teaching. (We will discuss this further later in the chapter.) However, Jung was closer than the usual visionary is to the essential experience because his images more closely reflect essence. The closer a person is to the essential presence, the more powerfully his images are influenced by it. When the person is directly in contact with essence, then the images become a more accurate reflection of it. When the imagination is grounded in the embodied experience of essence, the particular mentality has a less distorting effect on the images. Such images and visions can become so accurate that they are actual pictures of the essential state the individual is experiencing.

Here we move from the realm of visions to the realm of seeing. A person can develop an ability to see the essence directly, as it is. The imagination is not involved here. What is involved is the operation of an inner eye, a certain organ of perception that can see inner experience. The pictures are then clear. They have a definite meaning and significance and completely correspond with the direct experience of the presence of essence. This kind of experience is calm and steady, without the excitement and emotionality of visions. The person can look at essence and investigate it, as if he is using a telescope or a microscope. This is the "seeing" that Don Juan talks about in Carlos Castaneda's books. The individual is now a seer, not a visionary. The old sages of India were called seers because they had this essential faculty of seeing.

The more the individual is grounded in the embodied experience of essence, the more accurate his perception and the less it is influenced by the subjective mentality of his personality. The seeing, just like the presence of essence, can become a permanent presence, not an isolated happening. Whenever the person wants to see, he just looks.

There are other classes of mental experience that are customarily regarded as the experience of essence when in fact they are not, such as the experiences of insight and intuition. In psychotherapy, for instance, one might have an insight about oneself, about others, or about the nature of reality. It often occurs as a flash of illumination and is accompanied by a sense of expansion and certainty. Such insights can provide valuable information and affective satisfaction. Still, the experience of insight is not itself essence, not yet. An insight is an event, and essence is a presence. An insight is an experience of understanding a specific truth, whereas essence is an embodied presence, an ontological actuality.

Most of the time, insights give us liberating information and understanding of how our minds, emotions, and personalities function. They might even help lead us to essence. Insights can be liberating, profound, exhilarating, or powerful, but still they are not essence. Essence is more.

Insights can go even deeper, to more profound levels of reality, and can give us information about the nature of reality. But what *is* this reality? It is nothing but the reality of our true nature, our essence. At such times we are receiving insights about essence itself. For instance, an individual can have the sudden deep flash that "I actually exist," or an expansive insight that "Love is my true nature." These are insights about essence, realizing some of the truth about our real nature. But this activity itself is not exactly the presence of essence. It can reach essence and give glimpses of it, but if the person remains at the level of insight, essence will not be realized, embodied, or lived in its fullness and beauty.

As we see, insight is a certain happening or a certain capacity to get information and understanding. The object of insight can be anything; it can be one's mind, one's personality, or even one's essence. The deepest and most profound insights are those concerning the essence, when we start understanding our true nature. Finally, insight can be so profound that it becomes a direct perception of essence. We may get a glimpse, maybe just a flash, but it is a glimpse of essence. We have a momentary contact with essence. We *are* essence for that moment. But since it does not last long enough for us to investigate at ease, we are left with only the understanding, and we call this insight. It is literally insight (in-sight): seeing into the inside, into the essence. We can have the insight "I am actually made out of truth," a powerful insight that shakes the mind. However, such an insight is only a meager, limited glimpse of the presence of essence. It is a vastly important and profound insight about one's true nature, and it can actually change one's life, but it is not as complete as being the essence. Contrast the insight that "I am made out of truth" with the experience of the realized person who is continually experiencing essence and is always aware of its nature. Such a person can at length and at ease investigate the qualities of essence and can learn in specific details what truth is, what *being* truth means, what that does to the mind, what it does to the body, how it affects others, and how it can be used most efficiently for the benefit of all. Insights come all the time to the realized person. They are not isolated flashes. This person has the switch to the flashlight and can turn it on and off at will, for any duration and to any intensity or depth he chooses. This is a fact of the life of essence. So we see how taking insight as essence can be very limiting. Insight is useful; it can be used to contact essence itself. Then insights become the spontaneous flashes of essence.

Now let us look at intuition. The word *intuition* is used to describe many different kinds of perception, of varying depth, profoundness, and accuracy. Sometimes intuition can mean a suspicion of a certain truth, a slight glimpse without certainty or clarity. Sometimes intuition can mean a feeling, more or less vague, about something. If we listen to such a feeling, it can lead us to understanding. Sometimes intuition is a hunch, something like a guess but with more of a feeling of certainty or weight to it. These are some of the things we call intuition.

There are deeper aspects of intuition: for example, when we somehow know something, sometimes with a feeling of certainty, but don't know how we got the knowledge; we cannot explain to ourselves how we know. Sometimes we know something totally new, but we don't know where it came from, so we say we have an intuition. An intuition sometimes feels like a direct apprehension of a certain truth, but we can't explain how this apprehension occurred. So intuition is usually considered a mysterious process.

Like insight, intuition can be about anything—the mind, other people's personalities, relationships, and even our true nature, our essence. However, intuition itself is not essence. It can help us to know essence, but it is a process or a capacity, not an ontological existence.

The phenomenon of intuition can be illuminated by considering Sigmund Freud's statement that the unconscious knows everything. Our unconscious (in the sense that Freud used the term) knows everything about us and about others, but because it is unconscious, the information is not available to us. Sometimes, however, some of the content of the unconscious enters our consciousness in a way we can't explain. So we call this kind of awareness intuition. The feeling of not knowing where the hunch or intuition came from indicates that it came from the unconscious, a part of the mind that we are not usually in contact with. That's why intuition feels mysterious.

Knowing this, we can now understand the various kinds of intuition. According to Freud, the unconscious contains all the information about our minds, everything that has ever happened to us, and nothing that we go through escapes being recorded in the unconscious. This explains the intuition we get about our minds and the workings of our personality.

Freud also mentions that the unconscious knows everything about the other person in any relationship, including his unconscious, but he doesn't explain how. Obviously, this means that the unconscious has some kind of capacity to perceive things in others. We are then talking about empathy, telepathy, ESP, and so on.

However, let's put it in a simple way. Every part of the mind that the individual is not consciously in contact with is still present, but it is in the unconscious part of the mind. This includes not only the repressed part of the personality but everything that is repressed, including the essence and its capacities. Freud was referring to the personality and the mind when he talked about the unconscious. He didn't have the concept of essence. Here, we see that his insight naturally extends to the other parts of the individual, such as his essence. We will show in a later chapter that essence is repressed, just like everything else. Therefore, information can leak out from the unconscious not only about emotional complexes but also about the essence. That is why we have intuitions sometimes about essence. The unconscious knows the essence. All of the knowledge is there, but is not available to consciousness. And intuition is a way of having access to some of this knowledge without having the essence itself in consciousness.

Essence has many capacities, some of which are called the subtle organs of perception, which transcend the physical senses. These capacities, which transcend time and space and therefore the limitations of the physical senses, are in the unconscious. This explains how the unconscious knows about other people. So we see that intuition is not essence itself but can come from essence and can be used for the understanding of essence. However, when essence is present in the conscious experience of the individual, then there is no intuition and no mystery. There is just direct perception and direct knowing—direct knowing of essence because there is consciousness of it, direct perception of oneself and others because essence has the capacities that transcend the boundaries of time and space. You don't need to wait for intuition, you just look, just pay attention. You see, you perceive, you know. You know how you know. You understand the mechanism and the process. You can turn it on or off whenever you like. You can direct it wherever you want.

There is a deeper form of intuition that is the function of a certain aspect of essence. We referred to this aspect earlier as objective consciousness or the diamond body. We also called it the body of knowledge. This aspect has the capacity to take facts and data, all of the different kinds of understanding about a particular object or situation, and consider them all together, simultaneously and instantly. The reasoning mind is linear; it cannot consider too many facts at the same time to find a solution. It is limited in its capacity to hold information simultaneously. This is why computers are so valuable. They can consider a whole array of facts, all at the same time.

This aspect of essence can do just that, not in a thought form but in a more lived and felt way. Its capacity for considering many facts and many dimensions is limitless. Everything in the situation is considered, and the result is a certain perception that integrates all the facts, on the various levels of understanding.

If this part of us is unconscious, then we will experience its perception as an intuition. If it comes in a flash, we think of it as an insight. If this aspect of essence is present in our consciousness, we experience the perception as a direct knowing. This is real intuition. A person who is this essence does not need to use the linear mind and rack his brain over certain important situations. The direct knowledge is just there, available. There is usually a certainty with it, a clarity and precision, and also an aliveness that is very delicate and exquisite. This delicacy, this exquisite presence is missed when the person is satisfied with insights and intuitions and does not use them to guide himself to their source, which is essence.

ESSENCE AND THE HEART

Many people, especially those who look for their true nature through love and devotion, assume that essence is going to be some kind of emotional state. True, the emotional state sought is thought of as free, beautiful, full of love and joy—what is called an open heart. The search is for a wonderful feeling of bliss. So it is seen and expected as an emotional state.

This can be very tricky, because a feeling is closer to the experience of essence than is a thought or an image. And it is because of this proximity of feeling to essence that we need to be more awake and more precise in our understanding. Regardless of how beautiful, blissful, and deep emotions and feelings are, they are not essence. Essence is a different dimension of experience.

The main difference between emotional states and essence is that the former are discharged processes of our nervous systems, whereas the latter is definitely not. Emotional states are primarily physiological processes accompanied by some ideational content. On the other hand, essence is not a physiological process and is not a discharge of the nervous system. Essence is independent of the nervous system, transcends physiological processes, and can, in fact, exist without the physical organism. Essence, when it is present, affects the nervous system, but it is not the discharge, or the emotion, that results from the contact between essence and the physiology.

This is a very important difference. It means that emotions don't really exist except in the sense that activities exist. They are activities, and activities don't have an ontological presence. Essence, on the other hand, is not an activity. As we saw in chapter 1, essence is a presence, and its basic quality is its existence as an ontological actuality, as a "suchness." An emotion is an activity that starts and ends, whereas essence is a presence. An emotion is like the movement of water, the activity that is the motion. The motion of water is not the water. Water can be still, without motion. Essence, on the other hand, is like the water. It exists whether there is motion or not.

So the person who takes his positive emotions to be his true nature or essence is really missing the truth. Such a person will continue to develop the life of the personality, based on certain emotional states, rather than the life of the essence. But this is the ordinary condition of the unrealized person who is always looking for positive emotional experiences. And it is this very search for positive emotions that prevents most of us from realizing our essence, which transcends both positive and negative emotions.

Although we can see here the fundamental difference between essence and emotion, it is usually not easy, especially for the beginner, to tell the difference because they feel similar. The situation is further complicated by the condition of modern Western man, who is very alienated from his emotions. Many people do not even experience their emotions, and the ones who can do not usually experience them deeply or fully. The felt emotions are usually so distorted and dominated by negativity that it takes a lot of hard work to start feeling them both deeply and in a balanced way.

The people involved in many of the new growth movements and New Age therapies think of themselves as engaged in "personal growth," but they are usually thinking of emotional growth. This is usually true even when people think they are pursuing "spiritual development." Emotional satisfaction and positive emotional states are what they are actually seeking. And very often it is not emotional growth that they achieve but emotional discharge.

Now the capacity for emotional discharge is necessary for emotional growth and balance. Also, balanced emotional growth is necessary for finding and developing one's essence. However, the emotional life is still not the essential life. Here it is useful to look at the difference between the emotionally healthy, normal person and the realized person.

We know how impoverished the life of the emotionally blocked person is in comparison to that of the normal person who enjoys a full and deep emotional life. From the perspective of essence, the person with the deep and full emotional life is just as impoverished in his experience, compared to that of the essential individual, as is the emotionally blocked person compared to the healthy one— impoverished, in fact, by many more orders of magnitude. In the experience of the essential individual, the emotionally developed normal person is superficial, incomplete, and still a child in terms of the potential of the human being.

It is common, although not accurate, to say that essence is experienced as a feeling because it is felt and not thought. It is a felt experience but not a feeling. It is easy to understand this: we can feel our stomach, for instance, but our stomach is not feeling. The stomach actually exists. It is the same with essence: we can feel it, but it is not a feeling. It actually exists. But because essence is felt, and often produces effects in the body similar to the effects produced by emotion, and also because essence is not a physical presence, people tend to confuse it with emotions and feelings and hence never identify it as it is. We can put the matter in the form of a koan: What is the part of you that you can feel but is not part of your body and is not a feeling?

In terms of the language of some psychological schools, essence can be confused with affect. This is because essence has an affect, in the sense that it can feel soft, warm, gentle, smooth, hard, dense, and so on. But it is not the affect. These are some of its qualities but not its basic nature. A diamond is hard, but the hardness is not the diamond. So essence is like the diamond. It has qualities, just as the diamond has qualities of hardness, brilliance, and so on. The qualities of essence, then, can be called affects.

Although this is very clear and can be taken for granted by one who knows essence, it can be very confusing for others. To clarify further the difference between spiritual experience and the experience of truth, let us look at the case of a seeker after essence who is having profound, expansive experiences and revelations. Suppose this person comes to the state of the opening of the heart, with the subsequent flow of feelings of love, and of various blissful states.

This happens to many seekers who practice one of various meditation techniques and spiritual exercises.

At some point in the practice, the heart center opens, and the person is flooded with deep, intense feelings of joy and love. He feels transported. He has a sense of emotional freedom, sometimes accompanied by beautiful thoughts, images, or visions. The heart is full of love and compassion toward the self and others. Such a person might see lights of various beautiful colors and intensities. He might even feel he is made of light. He might realize "I am the light."

This is all beautiful and good. In fact, it is necessary for inner development. But this is not yet essence. This kind of experience is what usually happens when one of the *chakras* in the body is activated. *Chakra* is an Indian word meaning "center" or "wheel." The chakras are different centers of certain energies; the heart chakra is one of many. They are usually located at the main plexi of the nervous system and are very much linked with the nervous system and its processes. Their function is mainly the coordination of some basic physiological and autonomic discharge processes.

The energies of the chakras are the basic raw energies of emotional states. When a chakra is active, or "open," we directly experience the basic subtle energies that go into the makeup of the various emotions, instead of the emotions themselves. That is why we experience emotional freedom when the heart opens: the energy frees us, for the moment, from the conflicting emotions that usually fill our hearts. The basic energy of the heart chakra is experienced as love, joy, and bliss. When it is seen, it is seen as colored lights in the heart, usually golden or green.

The activation of the other chakras will have a similar sense of expansion, freedom, light, and so on but not necessarily love. In such openings there is generally a flooding of deep, intense emotions and feeling, usually experienced as a high-energy, dramatic happening. The person has the sense that it's a "big deal," that he is having a spiritual experience or a mystical union. This is true, but it is also true that this is only a transitory stage. All the drama subsides after a while, and other processes, subtler and deeper, begin to take place.

However, because the level of the chakras is dramatic, intensely emotional, and full of visions of all kinds of beautiful phosphorescent lights, it has a fascinating and captivating influence on the mind. The person keeps seeking these dramatic experiences and is not interested in the subtler processes that are necessary for moving to the essential dimension.

The drama and the flash are mostly the result of the emotional nature of the experience. Each chakra contains so many deep and intense emotions, which have been suppressed and stored up for many years, that when the chakra is activated the energies of all these dammed up emotions are liberated and flood the person's consciousness. The deepest emotions in the heart are those of love and joy, and they flood out in all their intensity, producing beautiful lights, sensations, and ecstatic states.

Chakra experiences, such as the experience of the heart opening, are considered by many systems of inner development as temptations. The seeker can become addicted to this dimension of experience and stop there, aborting the process of essential development. This addicting characteristic of the chakra dimension can be seen in people who are addicted to high levels of excitement. The energy of excitement is the same energy that operates at the chakra level. Some people are even addicted to fear. They seek fear by putting themselves in dangerous situations. Watching horror movies is another way people enjoy the addiction to fear. The energy of fear is the same as that of pure excitement; it is the energy operating on the chakra level when it is colored by adrenalin. So the addiction to excitement and fear is the same as the addiction to the dramatic experiences of the chakra realm. People who are addicted to fear enjoy it because it is the only way they know of to activate their chakras, to have access to those energies. Here we are not referring to those neurotic individuals who are plagued by fear and anxiety. We mean those who look for excitement in fearful situations.

The heart chakra, like every other opened chakra level, functions as an entrance into a deeper realm, the realm of the essence. This realm is a whole universe, the universe of essence. Taking the experience of the heart chakra as the end is like standing at the door of this universe and never entering. It is true that the door is open, but the door is not the essential universe. The door is beautiful, colorful, and fascinating, but it is only the ornamented entryway to a realm that surpasses anything else in beauty and significance. The energy of the chakra level is sometimes symbolized by a serpent, a cobra, the *kundalini*. This scintillating and mesmerizing image of the kundalini cobra, although beautiful and magnificent, is also used in many teaching stories to symbolize the guardian of a treasure, a guardian that must be vanquished before the hero can attain the treasure. The treasure is the essential realm. The serpent is the guard at the door to the treasure (essence), protecting it and preserving it. Yet this guardian must be vanquished and superseded if the hero is to attain the treasure and enjoy the essential life.

So the chakra level, the realm of the kundalini, is a stage of inner development, not the destination. It can be used to go further. The open heart chakra can be used to go to the experience of essential presence if the individual allows himself to look further, beyond the glitter and excitement, into the deeper, more tranquil, and subtler presence in the heart. In fact, it can happen that the experience of the heart opening results from a contact with essence in the heart. The presence of essence might, by itself, open the heart chakra. The ecstatic experience is not only emotional but also essential—in some cases, the essence is flowing out but is experienced emotionally. In other cases, the flow of essence is mixed with the emotional, chakra-level energy. When a person is captivated by the emotional aspect of the experience, he tends to miss the presence of essence and so misses the opportunity to go on to the deeper and richer realm of essence. However, if he stays present in the experience and objectively looks at its constituents, he might stumble on the essential presence. He then has the opportunity to experience the essential realm in its purity, without the diluting presence of emotions. The quality of experience in the heart will be now very different from that of the chakra level. The first deeper level beyond the heart chakra might be the first essential experience. This is one of the centers that the Sufis call *lataif*. These centers are sometimes called "organs of perception."

> In Ibn Arabi as in Sufism in general, the heart (qalb), is the organ which produces true knowledge, comprehensive intuition, the gnosis (ma'rifa) of God and the divine mysteries, in short the organ of everything connoted by the term "esoteric science" (ilm al-Batin). It is the organ of a perception which is both experience and intimate taste (dhawq)...
>
> Here we have to do with a "subtle physiology" elaborated "on the basis of ascetic, ecstatic, and contemplative experience"....

In short, this "mystic physiology" operates with a "subtle body" composed of psycho-spiritual organs.[1]

This particular one of the lataif, the heart center, is connected with the experience of compassion. At this level of experience, all of the excitement, glitter, and drama of the heart chakra is gone. Instead, what is experienced in the chest cavity is emptiness. The whole chest feels as if it is all gone. There is nothing left but a very clear, peaceful, and silent emptiness. It feels as if nothing is occurring there, yet it is open and lucid. If the person pays closer attention, it will become apparent that this peaceful emptiness is pervaded by a very fine and subtle presence, so fine and subtle that it is usually overlooked by the one having the experience. This fine and subtle presence pervading the emptiness of the heart is the latifa or the first manifestation of it. The person will experience a subtle but exquisite sense of compassion, for himself and all others.

But if the person pays even closer attention, he will see that there is no emotion, no emotional discharge at all. Then where does the compassion come from? The person will see that the subtle presence pervading the chest cavity has a particular quality that we can say is its affect. This quality can best be described as loving-kindness. However, if the person tries to see exactly what the quality of this presence is, he'll see that it is not exactly compassion or loving-kindness but that loving-kindness is the closest thing in our language that describes it. It has a sense of warmth, gentleness, virgin newness, like that of a newborn infant, but it also has an intrinsic pleasurable quality that is difficult to describe. We can say it is like pleasurable lumination. Much more can be said about this fine presence.

Calling it loving kindness is very close but not exact. The emotion of compassion, as it is normally felt, is actually the discharge of the nervous system under the impact of the presence of this subtlety. It is not the presence but the emotional response of the nervous system to it. It approximates the essential experience but fails to reach it. In this example, we can see very clearly the difference between the chakra experience and the essence experience (here on the lataif level). The chakra experience is a discharge process; the

---

[1] Henry Corbin, *Creative Imagination in the Sufism of Ibn 'Arabi*, trans. Ralph Manheim, Bollingen Series 91. Copyright © 1969 by Princeton University Press. Excerpt, p. 221.

essence is more our nature. The first is an activity; the second is an ontological presence.

In spiritual literature, the word *heart* is sometimes used to denote the heart chakra and sometimes to denote the heart center, the latifa that is called *akhfa*, "the most hidden." Sometimes it refers to another latifa, *qalb*, the one on the left side of chest. "The word qalb (heart) may be considered an anatomical localization of the organ which has to be awakened. Its position is where the pulsation of the physical heart is normally to be determined on the left breast."[2]

But sometimes, some teachers, mostly Sufis, use the word *heart* to denote essence itself, the presence of true nature, in all of its facets.

Many authors who write about inner development use the word *heart* without regard to the various meanings it has. This is not terribly important for the beginner, but after a while it is of decisive importance for the person's understanding to know in what sense it is being used. This could make the whole difference in the person's understanding and experience.

ESSENCE AND THE BODY

In this journey of breaking the idols that masquerade as essence, we come to the sphere of action, movement, and physical activity. Some people, usually in reaction to the feeling that emotional love is selfish or useless, come to conclude that real love is action. They assert that love, compassion, truth, harmony, and so on are the particular actions that an individual takes, that the presence of the emotion, or the expression of the affect, does not mean that there is real love unless there is an action that is useful.

This is very tricky. There is truth in this assertion, but this truth can be misleading because it is partial. It is true that the emotion of love or the expression of it does not necessarily indicate the presence of real essential love. Most of the time, the emotion or its expression is conditioned by the personality and its unconscious under-

---

[2] Idries Shah, *The Sufis*. Copyright 1964 by Idries Shah. Reprinted by permission of Doubleday & Company, Inc. Excerpt, p. 302

pinnings. Hence, it is selfish love, which *is* self-seeking and useless. Also, as we saw in the last section, emotion and essence are not the same. Emotional love is not essential love. It is a discharge process, whereas essential love is a real presence.

The essential aspect of love *can* be present sometimes without overt action. Action might certainly result and very often does, but it is not necessary for the experience. When essential love is present, then it is our nature. We are present. It is the presence of a certain facet or aspect of essence. If there is a need for action, it will be taken. If there is no need, no action will result. Love, here, is being. It is Being. Sometimes the action of essential love is just being—not action but inaction.

In fact, the most important and useful action of love is simply its presence. Essential love acts by its mere presence, but in a subtle and invisible way. There is no overt physical movement or expression necessary. The presence of essence, in any of its various aspects, is its primary action. We will leave to another occasion the topic of how essence acts and will content ourselves here with a quoted passage, part of what is called the "Sarmoun Recital," about the knowledge and presence of essence. "He who knows, and knows that he is: he is wise. Let him be followed. By his presence alone man may be transformed."[3]

The main point here is that essence is being. This being can be expressed through action. Action is real only if its source is essence. The most real, the most fundamental act is the presence of essence.

A certain action that is usually considered spiritual or essential is that of service. Many systems and teachings focus on service, as both the method and aim of their inner work. Service is seen as freeing because it is considered unselfish or selfless, for the self-centered attitude is taken to be the main barrier against inner development.

This again is very tricky, because if a person doesn't know essence, it is impossible to tell whether his action is selfish or selfless. This is because the emotional self acts mostly according to unconscious motivations. A person might think he is serving another, or humanity, or God, but very often he is serving an idea or ideal that is mainly determined by unconscious selfish concerns. A common example is the person who is always trying to be good, supposedly to

---

[3] Idries, Shah, *The Way of the Sufi* (New York: E. P. Dutton, 1970), 253.

serve God, but unconsciously he is trying to propitiate his superego, which he projects on his idea of God.

Also, saying that service is selfless action is vague, unclear, and not necessarily accurate. The existence of the emotional self or false personality does not negate the existence of a real self. In fact, the essence is the true self, although it is called by other names. So in this context, what does it mean to be selfish, and what does it mean to do service?

Let's say that for an individual who knows essence, service is the serving of essence. The essence could be one's own or somebody else's, the essence of humanity as a whole or the nature and essence of all of existence. So true service is not a matter of serving somebody else. It is not serving the false personality, one's own or others'. It is serving essence.

We see that real service can be done only by somebody who knows essence. Selfless service means action not centered around the false personality but centered around essence. In essence there is no selfishness because there is no defensive separateness between oneself and others. When an action serves one's essence, it automatically serves the essence of everybody else. So we can say that service is the true selfish action, the action that serves the true self. For the person who does not know essence, service should be guided by one who does know essence; otherwise it will most likely be an exploitation, either by one's own superego or by somebody else's.

Service is not a morally good action. It has nothing to do with morality. Service is the useful and necessary work or action that is needed for the realization and development of essence, without regard to boundaries of self and other.

Another category of action connected to inner development is that of discipline. Discipline is a basic ingredient in almost all schools of inner development. This is for several reasons. One reason is that the emotional, false personality tends to act and behave in a haphazard way, mainly in whatever way seems to help avoid any unpleasant truth. So without discipline it will tend not to do the work necessary for inner development because this work is largely a process of confronting unpleasant truths, at least at the initial stages. Discipline will force one to confront, and not avoid, the unpleasant truths and sensations necessary for the work of inner development.

Discipline is necessary for developing certain attitudes and capacities needed for the work on inner development. For example, it is needed to develop the capacity for paying concentrated attention. In addition, discipline is necessary to carry out the practices that a particular school or system prescribes. Many systems require the discipline of regular meditation.

Thus, many people end up with the conviction that discipline is necessary and useful for everybody at all times. This is obviously false; very often we find that a person is disciplined not for the work on inner development but because of the inner authority of the superego. The case of the obsessive-compulsive neurotic who rigorously and ritually disciplines himself and his time is well known. This is an extreme case that well illustrates how discipline can serve the false personality and therefore hinder inner growth. So discipline needs to be exercised with understanding of the individual personality and the person's specific, true, inner needs. The requirement for discipline for a given individual varies depending on the particular time and place and the phase of development. Differing amounts and modes of discipline are needed for the development of different essential qualities or capacities. For instance, the development of the will requires a different kind of discipline from that of objective consciousness. So we see that even in the case of discipline, the knowledge of essence is of primary importance, if not absolutely necessary. This applies to all kinds of discipline concerning time, space, diet, speech, expression, or movement.

This brings us to the consideration of systems of movement and posture. There are many of these systems, both ancient and contemporary, and many of them are in vogue these days. There are schools of yoga, martial arts, sacred dance, movement methods, body and posture alignment, and so on. We will not go into detailed consideration of each of them but will content ourselves with some general remarks.

The value of most of these systems has been amply demonstrated by the people involved in them. However, this does not mean they are necessarily useful for inner development or are expressions of it. Essence is such a deep phenomenon that a person can be very healthy physically, with seemingly graceful movements and perfect posture, and still know not an iota about how to be essentially himself. In fact, many people who are yoga experts, accomplished in martial arts, wonderful dancers, movement professionals, or body therapists are actually using their accomplishments to hide from themselves the emptiness and the lack of the presence of essence in their bodies. Some of these systems were developed by people who actually felt the absence of their essential core and tried to compensate for the sense of deficiency with a system of movement or posture. Some of these systems are such a close imitation of what would be there if essence were present that most people get fascinated and captivated by the system's beauty, elegance, logic, and power. This close resemblance can function, unfortunately, to impede the development of the essential core because of the placebo effect. This is especially true when a person uses the particular system to fill or cover up a personal deficiency.

This situation is common, but at the same time it does not invalidate such systems, even for essential development. Some of these systems can be used, and very fruitfully, for essential discovery and development if there is knowledge and awareness of essential presence. Gurdjieff used his movements for such purposes. He knew their purposes and effects precisely. Only someone who has the essential knowledge and development that Gurdjieff had can use them for the same aim.

In the case of systems of posture, it is easy to see that there is no particular posture or alignment that fits all people at all times. The posture assumed by the body when the essential aspect of merging love is present is very different from the posture spontaneously assumed when the essential aspect of expansive peace is present. Different yet is the posture assumed when solid will is present. The physical postures and movements are different in these three cases. The center of presence and contact is concentrated more in the heart for the first, in the head for the second, and in the belly for the third. Of course, all of the body is involved, but the center of experience is different in each case. In the first case, that of the heart center, the body has a more humble posture. The posture of majesty and grandeur is characteristic of expansive peace. When will is present, the body is and moves like a mountain, solid and grounded.

Now, we cannot say one of these postures is healthier, better, or more balanced than the others. If we do, we are only showing our ignorance and prejudice toward one aspect of essence over another.

We cannot take one posture that is characteristic of a certain state, regardless of how healthy and balanced it is, and try to impose it on the body regardless of what essential state it is in. This will only predispose the body toward this particular state and eliminate the further expansion of many other states that are just as valid and healthy.

From this perspective we see that the best conditions for the body are resilience and flexibility. It is not a matter of a certain structure, alignment, or skill but of flexibility and openness, the absence of restricting contractions. The ideal condition is that the body can freely accommodate and express in its postures the essence in its various states and conditions. This is the freedom of the body. This freedom cannot be known unless the essence is there, embodied, present in our bodies.

When this happens, then our posture and our movements radiate out from the presence of essence and are not determined by any programming coming from within or from without. This is the true freedom, joy, and pleasure of the body.

When the body cannot accommodate the presence of essence, a person might attempt to get the pleasure and freedom he seeks through involvement in various physical activities. But whatever pleasure results involves either tension, friction, exertion, discharge, or physical contact. These are good on their own merit, but they fail to reach the richness of essence in its qualities of pleasure. They don't come close to the sweetness, exquisiteness, smoothness, refinement, and delicacy of essential experience. In a sense, essence is pure pleasure, a pleasure that exists in itself, and not a reaction, a response, or a result of anything. Our true nature, in one of its many facets, is pure unadulterated pleasure and delight.

Essence and Energy

Now we come to the realm of the subtle energies. By now the reader might have formulated the idea that essence must be pure energy. If essence is not the mind, not the heart, and not the body, it must be the life energy. Many schools and systems say just that. The life energy is then given different names and designations, depending on the system. In the Indian tradition there is mention of *prana,* *kundalini,* and *shakti.* In the Chinese tradition there is *chi.* In the West, Freud formulated the concept of libido, and later Wilhelm Reich discovered what he called the orgone. These are just a few. And of course there are the more well known electromagnetic, chemical, and biological energies that operate in the physical organism.

Most of these systems and traditions ignore or even deny the assertions of the other systems. Sometimes they seem to be talking about the same thing and sometimes not. A person studying this subject usually either sticks to the formulations of one particular system or gets lost among the various formulations. But most of these people reach the erroneous conclusion that the deepest in us is energy, whatever form it is assumed to take.

The word *energy* is becoming a blanket term for the many people interested in inner development. It is being used to refer to many and various phenomena. Sometimes what is referred to is not energy at all but a totally other kind of phenomenon, such as motion, expression, force, power, momentum, event. This indicates ignorance and begets more ignorance. It results from the absence of precise knowledge and discrimination of what there is in our experience. The blanket term *energy* is also sometimes used to refer to a cluster or combination of factors, either one of which or none of which might appropriately be called energy.

The term *energy* is now a popular household word. It is becoming the all and everything of many systems of human development. People want to free their energy, feel their energy, express their energy, build their energy, develop their energy, refine their energy, and so on.

This again is a tricky situation. We find that the propensity of the human mind to take an ingredient that is important and necessary for a larger process and conclude that it is the aim of the process is again in operation here with regard to energy. Energy is an important ingredient, the consciousness of which is absolutely necessary for inner development. However, it is not the aim nor the medium of inner development. In other words, energy is not essence. More accurately, essence is not just energy. It has an energetic quality to it and can be mistaken for energy by the energy-oriented person, but seeing essence as energy is at the least limiting. It is more accurate to say that essence is the source of energy, that its presence in its various forms and manifestations brings out or frees our energies.

Essence is something fundamentally different, more substantial, and deeper than energy, whether it is electromagnetic, chemical, chi, prana, kundalini, shakti, libido, orgone, or whatever. However, all these energies must be experienced and freed for a person to be able to move into the realm of being, our essential and true nature. Processes and systems that use energies, like chi, kundalini, shakti, or any of the other energies, are useful for freeing the superficial layers of the organism so that the freed energies can be used for the inner work that will ultimately lead to the discovery and realization of essence.

The human organism has many levels or layers of energetic functioning, some of these interpenetrating the others. Most systems focus on one particular layer and use the energies of this layer for the work of inner development. A whole system is then formulated that describes and utilizes these particular energies, their centers, and routes in the body.

The Indian system, for instance, deals with the level of the chakras. As we have seen, the chakras work with the energy that is the raw material for emotional states. Hence, freeing the chakras is really freeing oneself from the dominance of emotions and their conflicts. Some of the other energies singled out are prana, kundalini, and shakti. Prana is the energy connected with breathing and hence with vitality. In fact, breath contains other subtle energies, mentioned by other systems.

Kundalini is the main energy that fuels the chakra system. It is connected with sexual energy, but it is sexual energy only when operating in the lower chakras. In the heart chakra, it is experienced as love; in the head chakras, it is experienced as light.

Shakti is the same energy but in a different form, that of power. It is experienced as having more of an electrical quality than kundalini. Prana, on the other hand, is experienced as a softer kind of energy than either. It is almost like liquid air. Kundalini and shakti have a certain phosphorescent and colorful quality and hence are more flashy and dramatic.

The energy of the chakra level, whether it is called kundalini, shakti, or prana, can be considered to be the energy of essence. In other words, just as essence has the aspects of will, love, consciousness, and so on, it has also the aspect of energy. When the chakra energy is pure, we realize that it is a self-existing energy. We have so far differentiated between essence and energy to emphasize the sense of beingness that is so distinct in essence but not manifested in energy.

The Chinese tradition, on the other hand, deals with the acupuncture meridian system and with chi, which is the energy operating at this level. This level is slightly deeper than the chakra system, although in certain parts of the body it overlaps it. The chi is experienced as a softer, cushiony kind of energy, that is less electrical and denser than kundalini or shakti.

The Sufi tradition uses the lataif system. This is somewhat deeper than either of the above energy systems. In fact, at this level it becomes more difficult to speak of energy. We can still use the term *energy*, but the lataif really operate with the lighter, more diluted forms of essence. We can say that the lataif level is the transition from the level of energy to the deeper level of essential presence.

In the body there is an overlap in some areas between the centers connected with the lataif and the other two systems. We discussed the relation between the heart chakra and the *latifa* (the singular form of *lataif*) of the heart center in the section on emotions. Another area of overlap is at the solar plexus. At this region there is a chakra connected to social interaction and the control of anxiety. In some sense it could be considered to be the "trapdoor" to the unconscious. However, deeper in the same region there is the latifa called *sirr*, or "mysterious." It is connected with the essential aspect of will. Although the two centers overlap, the two levels are quite distinct; even the colors connected with them are very different.

There are other levels and centers in the body, even deeper than the lataif, but they are no longer centers of energy. They have more to do with the operation of essential presence and manifestation.

In the West, the two main bodies of thought dealing with human energy are those of Sigmund Freud and Wilhelm Reich. We will discuss each of them in much more detail in a later publication and will content ourselves here with some general remarks. The Freudian school postulated the existence of two instinctual energies, libido and aggression. On the psychoanalytic level of discourse, the energies dealt with are on the level of the chakras. The aggression energy is the red energy of the self-preservation instinct, whose primary location is the first chakra at the perineum. Libido is the orange-red energy of the sexual instinct, whose primary source is the second chakra at the base of the spine. So these energies are really the same as kundalini or shakti energy but are not seen by Freudians in their most expanded pure forms.

The concepts of libido and aggression, however, were formulated as inferences from various experiences and observations and therefore are not exact designations of what actually exists in the organism. Hence, sometimes we find these terms used to refer to the essential levels that correspond, to some degree, to the first two chakras. For instance, aggression is sometimes the red latifa (spirit) at the right hand side of the body, which operates in issues of separation. Libido is sometimes the yellow (gold) latifa (heart) at the left side of the body, which sometimes operates in issues of merging and connection. We see these implications in the ego-psychologists Blanck and Blanck's understanding of libido and aggression:

> It would be far more accurate to refer not to infantile sexuality, nor even to maturation as proceeding through psychosexual phases, but rather to infantile need organized around the particular erotogenic zone when many needs, such as need for object connection and for separation, exist simultaneously. Such a view allows room to recognize libido in the broader sense of a drive to unite, rather than the narrower one of sexual drive, and, as we shall develop shortly, to regard the aggressive drive as a drive to separate rather than to destroy.[4]

Reich's concept of the orgone is really a general blanket term for many kinds of subtle energies. Reich discovered (really rediscovered) the existence of a subtle energy that is not electrical or chemical, which he believed to be the biological aspect of libido. He then saw it as universal and not just biological. From his description of it, we can see that sometimes he is referring to prana, sometimes to chi, sometimes to shakti, and sometimes even to essence itself. He

---

[4] Gertrude and Rubin Blanck, *Ego Psychology II* (New York: Columbia University Press, 1979), 34. © 1979, Columbia University Press. Reprinted by permission.

seems to have believed that there is one subtle energy, which he called orgone. It is a great discovery, especially because it occurred in the West. However, if we go along with Reich and assume that there is only one subtle energy, then obviously we will tend to restrict our perception and so fail to experience the greater expansion that can lead to the experience of essence. Also, not discriminating between the various forms of energy can be limiting. For instance, sometimes essence is experienced by a person doing Reichian body work, but the therapist takes it to be orgone energy, and hence it is not identified. This aborts the essential development. The term *streaming*, for instance, is used in Reichian terminology to mean the free flow of energy and body fluids especially after some armor blocks are dissolved. However, sometimes what the Reichian therapist observes as streaming is not the flow of energy or body fluids but the presence and circulation of essence itself. The following quote from Elsworth Baker, the president of the American Board of Medical Orgonomy, about orgastic freedom is an example: "The full orgasm depends on complete absence of holding in the organism. At a certain point, excitation grasps the whole personality and its increase is not subject to voluntary control. Having spread to the entire organism, it then concentrates in the genital area and a warm, melting sensation follows."[5]

This sweet, warm, melting sensation is not really just a sensation. It is the presence of a certain aspect of essence, what we call merging love or merging essence. It is the same aspect that Blanck and Blanck referred to as a drive to unite in relation to libido. It is the experience of merging and uniting. Therefore, seeing it as a sensation, as a streaming, or as a streaming of energy, is inaccurate. This inaccuracy limits the experience and blocks the way to the recognition of essence. The point here is that what is called bioenergetic streaming or orgonomic current are again blanket terms that cover many different and specific subtle energies and essential aspects. If the therapist can recognize the specific essential quality that is present, he may be able to see the psychological issues connected with it, which will help greatly in delving into deeper realms of experience.

---

[5] Elsworth F. Baker, *Man in the Trap* (New York: Farrar, Straus & Giroux, 1974), 84.

ESSENCE AND THE PERSONALITY

We have discussed briefly, in simplified terms, the relation to essence of the mind, the heart, the body, and the energies that animate the three of them. We have seen that there is a universal tendency to take the various manifestations and contents of these realms as the ultimate and deepest experience of the human being; whereas the deepest part, the deepest value in us is our essence, and not any of these manifestations. This discussion might give the impression that we are setting the realms of mind, heart, and body against the realm of essence. However, that is not our understanding and not our position. In fact, we have shown how the correct understanding of these realms of experience and their relationship to essence can lead ultimately to the realization and development of essence. Setting these realms of experience into their correct perspective with respect to essence can reduce the possibility of identifying with or getting stuck with them and can increase the probability of advancing to the realm of essential presence.

If this is the case, then from where does this seeming opposition and contradiction between those levels rise? The answer is actually well known: it is the opposition between the life of the personality and that of essence. By personality we mean the usual identifications of the individual, his self-concept, which is sometimes called the false personality and which is called in spiritual parlance the *ego*.

Ego in this sense is not the same as the ego defined by Freud. There is an overlap between the two concepts, but they are definitely two different concepts. The Freudian ego, for instance, has the functions of perception, motility, reality testing, and so on. These functions are not included in the term *ego* as used in spiritual and work literature. This latter ego denotes mainly the identification of the individual that gives him the sense of self or identity.

Psychoanalytic ego psychology, and specifically its object relations theory, has formulated in a very useful way how this sense of self or ego identity develops. Basically, what is called a self-representation develops through the organization of the early experiences of the individual from smaller units into larger, more comprehensive ones. This happens concurrently with the development of object representation.

Self- and object-representations are schemas that are enduring organizations, or structures, within the mind, which are the outcome of the several processes subsumed under the term organization—assimilation, accommodation, generalization, differentiation, and integration. These schemas change most rapidly over the first three or four years of life along with perceptual and cognitive development in general. They continue to be modified with subsequent developmental tasks and experiences, such as the assimilation of the changes of puberty into the self-representation. However, the basic structure of the self as a cohesive, integrated, and differentiated representation is laid down in the earliest years.[6]

So the self-representation (ego identity) depends on a particular structuring of all realms of experience into a cohesive whole. This implies the structuring of the contents of the mind, heart, and body experience into a specific, very stable, rigid organization. This, of course, will organize and structure the flow of all energies in the body, because "ultimately structure within the psyche comes down to organization within the central nervous system."[7] The resultant sense of psychological identity is very much adhered to and defended by the individual as the most precious and absolutely necessary possession and attainment.

It is this sense of self, the core of the personality, and the need to preserve and defend it, that is the main reason why we see the realms of mind, heart, and body as if in opposition to essence. The personality, and its sense of self, is the particular structure of these realms. This structure includes only these realms, and if the realm of essence is introduced into it, essence will have a disorganizing and disintegrating influence on it. The personality will have to oppose essence to keep its own coherence and survival.

Essence is the real person, the real and true self. The personality is called false because it is attempting to take the place of the essence. As we will see in the next chapter, the personality and the

[6] Althea J. Horner, *Object Relations and the Developing Ego in Therapy* (New York: Jason Aronson, 1979), 76.

[7] Althea J. Horner, *Object Relations and the Developing Ego in Therapy*, 77.

ego identity develop to fill the void resulting from the loss of essence in childhood. So it is really an impostor, trying to pretend it is the real thing.

As we said above, the realm of experience of the personality is that of the mind, heart, and body and the energies that fuel them. This is why people take these aspects of experience to be the real thing. If the personality did not make this assumption, it would have to recognize that it is not the real thing, it is not the center of our life. This is tantamount to the personality allowing itself to die. In fact this event, or more accurately the death of the personality's belief in itself as the real thing, is the exact condition necessary for the realization of essence, for essence to become the center of our existence.

So the opposition to the essence is really from the personality. The personality will do anything in its power to preserve its identity and uphold its domain. This tendency—or let's say, this need—is so deep, so entrenched, so completely the fabric of our identity, that only the person who has gone a long way toward establishing the essential life will be able fully to apprehend and appreciate this. This need is literally in our flesh, blood, bones, even our atoms. The power of the personality is so great, so immense, so deep, so subtle that the person who contends with it for a long time will have to give it its due respect. Its power is awesome. Its subtlety is unimaginable. Its intelligence is limitless.

To preserve its cohesion and its position as the center of our life, the false personality will do all kinds of things to throw dust in our eyes. One of these maneuvers, in fact its most fundamental characteristic, is identification with the contents of our minds, hearts, and bodies. These areas are within ego's realm, and it is master there. So it will be quick to assert, "I've got it—the real truth at last." Although it may make changes within its realm, it will try to keep the particular structure of the ego, and at deeper levels it will stick to the familiar fields of experience.

When we get to the pure subtle energies, it will naturally make its most vehement effort to keep us at that level of experience, for if we go beyond that level to the realm of essence, then its structure, its very foundation, and the very reason for its customary mode of existence will start crumbling. The anxieties and fears encountered at this point are enormous, all-pervasive, and subtle. The individual will want to stop, at the same time congratulating himself, of course, for having arrived.

ESSENCE AND THE VOID

As we have seen, the personality is a certain structure, more or less rigid, that organizes our experience under the aegis of a sense of identity. This psychic structure is based on the process of identification. When a person believes he is an angry person, he is identified with anger. He cannot see himself as separate from the anger. The personality is nothing but a particular organization of very basic identifications of early childhood, or as Freud puts it, "The ego is formed to a great extent out of identifications which take the place of abandoned cathexes by the id."[8]

Essence, on the contrary, has nothing to do with identification. It exists purely as itself. There is no identification with past experience or any self-image at all. In fact, its presence is concomitant to the absence of identification with any self-image or psychic structure. When we are identified with a self-image we acquired in the past, we are not being our true nature. This means that for the realization of essence the first step is to disidentify, to see that we are not whatever self-image (self-representation) we have, that we are not whatever content we find, physical, emotional, or mental. This loosening of identification will loosen the rigid structure of the personality. More space will be created within us.

The final outcome of the process of disidentification is the experience of the dissolution of the psychic structure or self-image. This is the experience of space, of what is sometimes called the void—when self-image is dissolved, the person will experience the loss of boundaries, both physical and mental. The nature of the mind is then revealed as an emptiness, a void, an immaculately empty space. The void and the absence of the identifications that form the psychic structure are the same thing.

There are various depths and levels of empty space. We can say that the beginning of the void is the absence of identification with

---

[8] Sigmund Freud, *The Ego and the Id* (New York: W. W. Norton, 1960), 38.

the self-image. There is self-image but there is no identification with it. What results is the inner sense of expansion and spaciousness. Then, at a deeper level, the self-image is gone, dissolved. There is only the experience of empty open space, which is boundless, clear, and crisp. The focus is not on the content of the mind but on the spacious emptiness that is its nature.

However, this is not yet the deepest level. There might still be identification with an image, but unconsciously. Parts of the self-image might remain in the unconscious. These will surface, in time, and the experience of space will be lost. Disidentifying with these aspects of the self-image until they dissolve will deepen the experience of space.

So we see that the experience of the void does not necessarily require the end of self-image or of the personality. It means only that during the experience the personality is not there, is not running the show. This experience is of the utmost importance, for it shows us that we are not the personality. It creates room for expansion and essential development.

Many authors on inner development write about the void, or ego death, as if it were one definite experience that ends the ego identity once and for all. This is false and misleading. Ego death is a repeated, and in time a continual, experience. The void is a repeated and deepening perception. Writing about it as if it were one definitive experience that will completely end the individual's identification, and the accompanying suffering, in one shot is not only inaccurate, it is irresponsible and cruel. It will prejudice the student of inner development to seek a perfection or a kind of completeness that is unrealistic and will only add to the attachment to the identifications and to the already existing suffering.

Every realized human being continues to work on inner development. There is no end to the development and unfolding of essence. This development proceeds by exposing more and more, perhaps in time very subtle aspects of the personality. After the basic identification with personality is broken, the process of dissolving the subtler aspects of the self-image usually becomes easier. It is a continual dissolution of the boundaries of self-image, resulting in more expansion. It is not that personality is gone and now essence develops. It is rather that the more essence develops, the more personality is exposed and its boundaries dissolved. The fulfillment

and expansion of essence is endless and boundless. Those who
forget this should heed the words of the fourteenth Dalai Lama of
Tibet. He was asked in an interview:

> During the course of your own life, what have been your
> greatest personal lessons or challenges? Which realizations
> and experiences have had the most effect on your growth
> as an individual?

> DL: Regarding religious experience, some understanding
> of shunya—some feeling, some experience—and mostly
> bodhichitta, altruism. It has helped a lot. In some ways, you
> could say that it has made me into a new person, a new man.
> I'm still progressing. Trying. It gives you inner strength,
> courage and it's easier to accept situations. That's one of the
> greatest experiences.[9]

By *shunya* the Dalai Lama means the void. So we can see how a
highly realized being, considered by his tradition to be the incarna-
tion of Avalokiteshvara, the Bodhisattva of Infinite Compassion,
speaks of his continuing development. It is true that he is being
humble here, but he is beyond false humility. He is being compassionate, stating things as they are. Suffering decreases, but progress continues. Progress is expansion. Expansion means transcend-
ing more boundaries.

The experience of the void is an important juncture. It is
necessary for the transition from the realm of the personality to the
realm of essence or being. But by no means is it the final end of all
personality. And the void itself is not essence yet. The void is a
transition point. It indicates the absence of identification, the absence of self-image. This is absolutely needed for the discovery and
the establishment of essence, but it is not essence yet, and it is not the
end. The void is the absence of the personality, but as we have seen,
the essence is a poignant presence. The void is the absence of
identification, which forms the self-image.

It is true that the void is the main focus of Buddhism and of
Buddhist teachers. In fact, its emphasis on the void is the most

---

[9] John F. Avedon, *Interview with the Dalai Lama* (New York: Littlebird Publications,
1980), 20–21. Used by permission.

important contribution of Buddhism to the understanding of inner development. Buddhism has contributed more than any other system or tradition to the understanding of the personality and its dissolution in the experience of the void. Other systems talk about this experience as ego death, and most systems, such as that of the Sufis, talk about the *baqa*, the remaining after extinction, the existence after dissolution. The extinction of the personality is seen as a stage preceding that of the existence of essence.

So why do Buddhists not talk about essence? They do, and some of their books are mainly about essence and its development. Many Buddhist techniques are for the development of essence. However, the void, the absence of identification and conceptual identity, is stressed, and only the void is mentioned to students for a long period of time because of a certain understanding that dictates their approach to inner work. This understanding concerns the personality and its self-concept, which is seen as the main barrier to inner freedom and development. Also, the phenomenon we discussed above—the personality's tendency to use any content of experience to reinforce its presence—is dealt with by the Buddhist method of detachment from the content of experience until the emergence of the void.

The advanced Buddhist teachers understand that the void is a necessary transition to the life of essence, of being. That is why in Buddhism there is the term *Shunya* or *Shunyata* for the void, but there are other terms, such as Buddha nature, *Bodhichitta, Dharmakaya*, and many others, that refer to the experience of essence, and not to the void. Buddha nature is seen as our true nature, and there is no assertion that it is Shunyata. Bodhichitta means the nature or essence of the mind. Dharmakaya means being, absolute being, being-as-such. And what we here call *essence* is our being, our beingness.

Herbert Guenther, writing about Buddhist Tantra asserts: "The goal of Tantrism is to be, and the way to it may be called a process of self-actualization."[10]

In the same book, quoting a Tibetan Buddhist treatise, he says: "All sentient beings possess the nature of Buddhahood, continuously present since its beginningless beginning. What is this

[10] From *The Tantric View of Life*, p. 118, by Herbert V. Guenther, © 1972. Reprinted with permission of Shambhala Publications, Inc., Boulder, CO.

nature of Buddhahood? It is the existential fact and presence of mind; since it is intrinsically pure [it is] the beginningless time-encompassing dimension of Being (Dharmadhātu) unbroken, impartial, radiant in itself, as the pristine existential experience of Being (Dharmakāya)."[11]

It is generally attributed to Buddhism that the belief in the nonexistence of self, the void, is the deepest nature of reality. The presence and existence of essence is denied by most Buddhist students. But as we have said, this is a methodological point, and Buddhism does not negate the presence of essence or true self. A story about the Buddha will give his point of view:

"Tell me, O Enlightened One, is there a Self?"
The Buddha kept silent.
"Is there, then, no Self?"
He did not reply.
Vacchagetta rose and left. The noble Ananda asked the Buddha, "Why, lord, did you not answer Vacchagetta's questions?"
"Supposing, Ananda, I had replied that there is a Self, that would have meant siding with those ascetics and Brahmins who describe themselves as Eternalists. If I had replied that there is no self, that, Ananda, that would have meant siding with those ascetics and Brahmins who class themselves as Annihilationists. I have constantly held that all things are not Self—would it have been right on my part then to have told Vacchagetta there is a Self? And if I had replied that there is not a Self, wouldn't this have confused him even more? He would have gone away saying to himself, "I believed in a Self. What is there left for me now?"[12]

This story shows that Buddha was more interested in teaching than in asserting anything about a self. The Buddhist position becomes understandable if we see that there are two selves: what we

---

[11] Herbert V. Guenther, *The Tantric View of Life*, 124.

[12] D. Lal, trans., *The Dhammapada* (New York: Farrar, Straus & Giroux, 1967), 20–21.

call the false personality, on one hand, and the true self or essence, on the other. In the interview we referred to above, the Dalai Lama says:

> There are two types of "I" or Self: coarser and more subtle. There is the "I" which is designated on the gross mind and body and that which is designated on the subtle mind and energy. When the one is active the other is not. The coarse "I" is designated in dependence on the coarse mind and body. But even when they are not operating, there has to be an "I" designated. That is then designated to the subtle mind and body which are then present. For instance, a highly developed yogi who is able to manifest a subtler consciousness and at the same time view conventional phenomena, for that person there is an innate sense of "I"—not in the coarser sense, but in a far more subtle sense—designated upon the subtle mind and body.

* * *

> JA: What happens to the most subtle energy-mind when a being becomes enlightened?
>
> DL: The "I" of a Buddha, the self of a Buddha, is this subtle "I."[13]

The venerable Trungpa Rimpoche, one of the foremost representatives of Tibetan Buddhism in the West, makes it very clear that the void or Shunyata is not the end experience:

> The shunyata experience corresponds to the level of a bodhisattva. But the shunyata experience is in a sense incomplete from the point of view of the next stage, which is the experience of prabhasavra, luminosity. Prabhasavra is the ultimate positive experience. Shunyata is like the sky. That space of the sky being there, it becomes possible for cosmic functions to take place within it. It becomes possible for there to develop sunrise and sunset. In the same way,

---

[13] John F. Avedon, *Interview with the Dalai Lama*, 63–64. Used by permission.

within the space of shunyata, of openness and freedom, it becomes possible for students to begin to deal with the actual experiences of non-duality. This is the prabhasavra experience, which is a way of acknowledging the Buddha-nature that exists within one.[14]

Luminosity is the essence, or the beginning of the experience of essence. Here we see very clearly that the void is seen as an important and necessary step before the perception of our Buddha nature, our being, our luminous essence. At least, the presence of the void does not negate the presence or the reality of essence.

Bhagwan Shree Rajneesh, a contemporary Indian teacher, expresses the relationship between the personality, the void, and essence, even more graphically:

> The Void is void in the sense that nothing of you will be left then; but the Void is not void in another sense, because the whole will descend in it—the Void is going to be the most perfect, fulfilled phenomena. So what to do? If you say "Void," suddenly the mind thinks there is nothing; then why bother? And if you say it is not void, it is the most perfect being, the mind goes on an "ambition-trip": how to become the most perfect being—then the ego enters it.
>
> To drop the ego the word "void" is emphasized. But to make you alert to the fact that the Void is not really a void, it is also said that it is filled with the Whole.
>
> When you are not, the whole existence comes into you.
> When the drop disappears, it becomes the ocean.[15]

So we see that the void is the emptiness resulting from the dissolution of the personality needed for the emergence of essence. In other words, the basic ground of our experience is empty space, the void. This space is usually filled by the personality and its identifications so that there is no room for essence. So there is a need for a clearing process, which will ultimately result in the emergence

---

[14] Herbert V. Guenther and Chogyam Trungpa, *The Dawn of Tantra* (Berkeley, CA, and London: Shambhala, 1975), 35.
[15] Bhagwan Shree Rajneesh, *Only One Sky* (New York: E. P. Dutton, 1976), 66–67. Used by permission.

of empty space. Then essence can emerge, and it will be the fullness of our being. It will take its place, as the source, the life, and the fulfillment.

ESSENCE AND SUBSTANCE

If essence is not an insight, an intuition, an emotional state, a subtle energy, or even the void, what is it then?

It is something that is much more wondrous than any of these, much more beautiful, much more magnificent, and much more meaningful. It is the only thing that will completely quench our hearts and the only thing that will be our peace of mind. Its existence is miraculous, and its characteristics are sheer delightful magic.

It is hidden within us, yet it is not part of its nature to be hidden, secret, or esoteric. Its truth is hidden because of its unlikelihood. We do not see or recognize it because we don't expect it; we always look for something else. We always look, and naturally so, for something that fits our usual categories of experience. We cannot imagine that there can exist a reality that is not mental, emotional, or physical. We are bound by our beliefs about what can be. So we miss, we ignore our essence, our true nature, without which we cannot really know what it is to be a genuine human being.

We are saying that essence is simply there, as us—not hidden, not secret, not complicated. It is staring us in the face, but our eyes go to something else, our minds reach far away. And we remain thirsty and discontented.

When we say essence is within us, we do not mean it is contained within our body the way a liquid is contained in a bowl. This will make essence and the body of the same nature, physical matter. However, we can come close to understanding the relation between our organism and essence by seeing the relationship between our body and space.

It is in the nature of physical space that it can coexist with the body. The body occupies a region of space, but this is not like the liquid in the bowl. The body does not displace space. The body and space overlap and occupy the same place. This is because they exist in different dimensions. Physical space and physical matter can occupy the same location because they are two different dimensions of existence.

It is the same with essence and the body. Essence is within us just as space is within us. It is on a different dimension from the body. Essence is a different order of existence from the body, and it is in this sense that it is within us.

Yet this analogy fails to do justice to the actual relationship between essence and the body. Because we usually think of space as a nonexistence, we find it easy to imagine space and the body coexisting in the same location. However, essence is not a nonexistence. It is not empty the way physical space is. It is, on the contrary, a fullness. It is something much more substantial than space. It has a substantiality similar to the physical body but in a different dimension.

In fact, essence is experienced as a kind of a substance but on a different order of existence from physical matter. Idries Shah, the Sufi author, describing the essential aspect of spirit, states: "According to Sufism, what is generally referred to in religious terminology as the Spirit (el ruh) is a substance, with physical characteristics, a subtle body (jism-i-latif)."[16]

Essence, when experienced directly, is seen to be some kind of substance, like water or gold, but it is not physical substance like physical water or gold. This is a very difficult point to make. Essence is experienced as a substance, a material. It has characteristics such as density, viscosity, texture, taste, and so on, but at the same time it is not a physical substance. It belongs to a different realm of existence. That is why it is called subtle. Some authors call it subtle matter, to distinguish it from the ordinary physical matter. "Here the importance is felt (as we have been reminded many times) of the world of subtle matter, mundus imaginalis (alam al-mithal), in the cosmology professed by all our Spiritual seekers. 'Subtle matter' is the esoteric Heavens of the heart, its 'astral mass' and so forth."[17]

It is not subtle in the sense that a thought is subtle compared to the body. It can be just as substantial as the body, as dense as solid gold. It is this truth of essence, its substantiality, that is unexpected

---

[16] Idries Shah, *The Sufis*, 395.

[17] Henry Corbin, *The Man of Light in Iranian Sufism* (Boulder, CO, and London: Shambhala, 1978), 108.

by the ordinary person. This is the unlikelihood that makes it mysterious and hidden. El-Ghazali, the famous Sufi of the Middle Ages, using the words *heart, spirit*, and *soul* interchangeably, says it is "a mysterious divine substance which is related to the material heart like the relation between the dweller and the house or the artisan and his implements. It alone is sentient and responsible."[18]

The term *substance* is sometimes used in a figurative way. We say that somebody has substance or that an idea has no substance. The first usually means that the individual has an inner reality or nature that makes us aware of a depth and weight to him that is almost palpable. But where did the expression of having substance come from? Why is the word *substance* used? The Merriam-Webster dictionary defines it as "1a: essential nature: ESSENCE b: fundamental or characteristic part or quality. c: *Christian Science*: SPIRIT. 2a: ultimate reality that underlies all outward manifestations and change."

We see that the original meaning of substance is essence, the way we have used the term. The dictionary goes on to give the other meaning of substance as physical matter. So even the language reflects the link between essence and substance.

Most likely, the origin of the expression "He has substance" is the actual knowledge of the nature of a human being as a kind of substance that gives depth and significance. When an individual is in touch with his essence, he literally has substance. The expression here is not figurative, although it is usually used figuratively now that most people have forgotten the original meaning, the literal one. We can see here how the expression originated and how the figurative meaning is related to the original meaning. Originally, having substance meant having one's nature, which is a kind of matter. The literal and figurative meanings were the same. This happens frequently in the development of language; we end up with the figurative meaning, devoid of the wisdom of the original expression.

This is true also of the other expression, that an idea has no substance. It is easy to see now how this expression originated. An idea that has substance is an idea that literally originated from substance, the substance of essence. It is an idea that expresses a

---

[18] The Sirdar Ikbal Ali Shah, *The Spirit of the East* (London: Octagon Press, 1973), 136.

truth of essence and hence is pregnant with meaning and significance. An idea that has no substance is an idea with no deep meaning, no reality, no truth. The reality is obviously, in the original usage of the expression, the truth of essential experience.

There are expressions like these, relating to substance, in many languages, which indicates an original knowledge of essence as substance. We usually understand the word *essence* in terms of the inner nature or the pure inner quality of something. The Merriam-Webster dictionary defines essence as "1a: the permanent as contrasted with the accidental element of being. b: the individual, real, or ultimate nature of a thing."

Here it stays on the figurative level; the pure inner quality could be anything. That is why we can use the word *essence* to refer to our human inner nature. But how did the word *substance,* which usually means matter, come to refer to the same thing as essence, as we saw above in the dictionary definition? Obviously, there must have been in the origin of language the knowledge of essence or inner nature as substance.

This perception and understanding of essence as substance is so significant and so fundamental that in most instances it makes the whole difference between self-realization and its absence. It is of utmost importance to remember that the word *substance* is used here literally and not figuratively or metaphorically. This understanding has monumental significance for self-realization and enlightenment. For the individual who recognizes essence as a substance with physical characteristics, self-realization will happen naturally and spontaneously. When essence is recognized, it starts to live and function, and this will bring about the whole essential development because it is the nature of essence to move to deeper and deeper realms. That is why Sufism, for instance, is understood as the gathering and collection of a certain *baraka* (blessing) or substance. "In neutral phraseology it could be said that the Sufis believe that Sufic activity in producing a Complete Man accumulates a force (substance) which itself is capable of alchemicalizing a lesser individual."[19]

The person who does not understand this fact and fails to recognize essence in its substantial nature will find it extremely difficult to move more deeply into himself and will stay on a level of

---

[19] Idries Shah, *The Sufis,* 294.

existence that falls short of being a genuine and complete human being. This is not dogmatism; the substance is the essence, and if the person does not recognize it, then he is not recognizing his true nature. The Sufis in fact see this substance as the true nourishment for humanity, and as the force that is needed even for its physical existence and continuation.

Idries Shah puts it in the words of Israil of Bokhara:

"The teaching is like air.

"Man dwells in it, but cannot realize by real feeling that but for it he would be dead. . . .

"He may become aware of it, and profit more from it, by realizing that it is a common substance treated with such heedlessness that nobody observes its presence."[20]

The substance of essence is equated here with the teaching, for any real teaching is nothing but the exterior manifestation of essence.

Many of the Sufis had also equated true knowledge with essence: "Gazali shows that the element which the Sufis call 'knowledge' is employed as a technical term, and that its functions for the human being go far beyond what one would ordinarily regard as knowledge. . . . Sufi knowledge, therefore, is something which continually pours into man."[21]

The fact of essence as substance, of the knowledge as substance, is the basis of the Sarmoun brotherhood, which some people regard as the heart and inner source of the Sufi orders. "There are many legends about the Sarmoun Darqauh ('Court of the Bees') and one of them is this. True Knowledge, it is asserted, exists as a positive commodity, like the honey of a bee. Like honey, it can be accumulated."[22] The knowledge that is collected like honey is the substance of essence itself. It is the source of true knowledge, and it is the knowledge itself. Or we can say it is the body of knowledge.

Gurdjieff recognized the truth of essence as substance, and built his system around it. That is why he made the various maps and

---

[20] Idries Shah, *Thinkers of the East* (London: Jonathan Cape, 1971), 26.

[21] Idries Shah, *Thinkers of the East*, 177.

[22] D. M. Martin, "Account of the Sarmaun Brotherhood," in *Documents of Contemporary Dervish Communities*, ed. R. W. Davidson (London: Society for Organizing Unified Research Cultural Education, 1966), 23.

gradations and used H (hydrogen) as standing for subtle and essential energies. He says:

> The next idea which it is necessary to master is the materiality of the universe which is taken in the form of the ray of creation. Everything in this universe can be weighed and measured. The Absolute is as material, as weighable and measurable, as the moon, or as man. If the Absolute is God, it means that God can be weighed and measured, resolved into component elements, "calculated," and expressed in the form of a definite formula.[23]

As we see, this fact of substantial essence has been recognized by the Sufi tradition and utilized for its methods of work. In addition, this truth is known by all genuine systems of inner development. It is usually not publicly emphasized and not much written about because most publications concern the preparation for and the first steps of inner work, before the actual self-realization, before the embodiment of essential substance. Nonetheless, we find strewn in the literature many references to the nature of essence as substance. For the individual who does not know the fact of substantiality, these references are either ignored or taken figuratively, or because they are puzzling, they are taken to contain some secret or esoteric knowledge that is difficult to understand. The literal and most obvious meaning is missed.

It is our understanding that many authors do not emphasize or single out the fact of substantiality because they themselves are not fully aware that this substance within them is itself the transforming agent, is itself the being. They are aware of the result, which is the freedom and the joy they experience. This is very likely to happen because it is possible and easy to confuse this unique substance of essence with the various substances that flow in the body. The body has many substances and fluids flowing in it; thus, when essence is experienced, it might not be recognized as having a different nature. It can be mistaken for just another substance of the physical organism, such as the blood or the cerebrospinal fluid, for instance. But most commonly it is mistaken for a feeling or a flow of sensations or energy, or "streaming" as the Reichians say. Of course, this error

---

[23] P. D. Ouspensky, *In Search of the Miraculous*, 86.

is supported by the already existing preconception that there is no such thing as a substance that is not physical matter.

We believe that there is also the reason of caution taken by some authors. If a seeker hears that essence is a substance, and if the tendency of the individual's personality toward identification for the purposes of defense is still dominant, there might arise the error of taking an unidentified sensation or a physical substance of the body as the essence. This sort of error can lead to negative consequences. So we need to state here that knowing that essence is a substance does not make it easier to perceive. The process of self-realization will still require all the work of understanding and refinement of perception.

On the other hand, the knowledge of substantiality can work as an orienting force, a confirming insight, a safeguard against not recognizing or ignoring essence when it might be present, and a protection against taking something else to be our true nature and essence.

We believe it is time to make this truth as clear, as precise, and as available as possible. It can save many people much hardship and waste of time and effort. There is no need for this knowledge to continue to be secret and esoteric, especially now that there is a tremendous need and thirst for it. We can use understanding and clarity to safeguard against misusing it.

The old idea that the personality must be loosened almost completely before essence is realized has to be modified in light of the latest findings. The old idea is that the personality is the barrier and must be removed before there can be a recognition of our essential beingness. Our findings indicate that essence can be realized in steps or in degrees, simultaneously with work on the personality. Each essential aspect or facet has a psychological constellation associated with it. This association is universal to all people. Understanding and resolving the relevant psychological constellation (which is only a sector of the personality) will allow the associated aspect of essence to emerge in consciousness. It is not necessary to resolve the personality as a whole. That is the subject of Chapters Three and Four of this book, in which we describe methods that enable a person to recognize essence in a much easier and faster way than has been possible with the old methods. Such techniques use essence itself as a help in understanding and resolving the rigidity of the personality. This is a new method, which we call the Diamond Approach. It is the subject of Chapter Four of this book.

The point here is that we don't need to go the laborious way of first bringing about the complete death of ego identification and then working on essential development. In fact, we can use essence itself in a very effective way to bring about the total dissolution of ego identifications. This point makes very obvious the need and usefulness of identifying and recognizing our essential substance.

So far we have given quotations referring to the substance of essence only from Sufi sources. The reader might be led to believe that this must be a Sufi phenomenon or concept. That is far from the truth. We have used Sufi sources because they are the clearest and the most definite in regard to this understanding of essence. Nevertheless, all the major genuine systems have this understanding, although for one reason or another it is not pointed out clearly or directly.

From the Hindu tradition, we can see this understanding very clearly spelled out in the works and writings of Sri Aurobindo, who was born in Calcutta on August 15, 1872. He very clearly understood that this substance is the essence, the agent of transformation, and the truth. He saw it as a force with a mass, which descends from the head at the first encounter. That is why he called it the descending force:

> To begin with, when peace is relatively established in the mind, failing absolute silence, and when our aspiration or our need has grown, has become constant, piercing, like a hole within, we observe a first phenomena which has incalculable consequences for all the rest of our yoga. We feel around the head and more particularly in the nape of the neck, an unusual pressure which may give the sensation of a false headache. At the beginning we can scarcely endure it for long and shake it off, we seek distraction, we "think of something else." Gradually this pressure takes a more distinct form and we feel a veritable current which descends— a current of force not like an unpleasant electric current but rather like a fluid mass. We find then that the "pressure" or the false headache at the start was caused simply by our resistance to the descent of the Force, and that the only thing to do is not to obstruct the passage (that is, block the

current in the head) but to let it descend into the strata of our being from top to bottom. This current at first is quite spasmodic, irregular, and a slight conscious effort is necessary to get reconnected with it when it is blurred; then it becomes continuous, natural, automatic, and it gives the very pleasant sensation of a fresh energy, like another breath more ample than that of our lungs, which envelops us, bathes us, lightens us and at the same time fills us with solidity.[24]

Its characteristics are described, referring clearly and exactly to its substantial qualities:

As his concentration grows stronger by "active meditation," by his aspiration, by his need, he will feel that this surge inside him begins to live: "She widens bringing out that which lives," says the Rig Veda, (I. 113–118), "awakening someone who was dead"—that it gathers a more and more precise consistency, an ever denser strength and, above all, an independence, as if it were at once a force and a being within his being. He will notice, first of all in his passive meditation (that is, when at home, calm, with eyes closed), that this force in him has movements, a mass, varying intensities, and that it rises and descends within him as if it were not steady—much like the shifting of a living substance; these inner movements can even gather a strength sufficiently great to end the body when the force descends or to straighten it up and draw it back when it rises. In our active meditation, that is, in the ordinary external life, this inner force becomes more diluted and gives the sensation of a small muffled vibration in the background, as we have already seen; besides, we feel it is not only an impersonal force but a presence, a being in our depths, as though we had a support there, something that gives us solidity, almost a backbone, and a quiet outlook on the world. With this little vibrating thing within, one is invulnerable and no longer alone. It is then everywhere, it

---

[24] Satprem, *Sri Aurobindo* (Pondicherry, India: Sri Aurobindo Ashram Trust, 1968), 38–39. Used by permission.

is there always. And strangely enough, when one has discovered it, it is the same thing everywhere in all beings, in all things; there can be a direct communication as though it were exactly alike, without a wall. We have touched then something in us which is not a toy of universal forces, not the thin and dry "I think therefore I am" but the fundamental reality of our being, ourself, truly ourself, the true center, warmth and being, consciousness and force.

As this surge or this inner force takes on a distinct individuality, as it grows indeed as a child grows, the seeker will become aware that it does not move at random as he had thought at first, but that it gathers itself at various points of his being according to the activities of the moment and that really it is this force which is behind each centre of consciousness: behind the mental centres where one thinks, wills, expresses himself; behind the vital centres where one feels, suffers, desires; or lower, or higher; and that it is truly this which knows—all the centres including the mind are only its openings on the different states of the universal reality or its instruments of transcription and expression.[25]

We see that Aurobindo not only understood that this substance or force is the essence, the being, but that it is the transforming agent and also the knower and force behind all centers. Aurobindo found confirmation for his experience and understanding in the old Vedic books of India, particularly the ancient Rig Veda.

The Mother, Aurobindo's associate and successor, describes essence in very beautiful and clear words: "To find the soul one must step back from the surface, withdraw deep within, and enter, enter, go down, far down into a very deep hole, silent, still; and then down there, is something warm, tranquil, rich in contents, and very still, and very full, like a sweetness—this is the soul."[26] We notice here that the Mother is describing essence in the aspect of sweet merging love, which we mentioned earlier.

---

[25] Satprem, *Sri Aurobindo*, 60–61.
[26] Satprem, *Sri Aurobindo*, 91

Another recent Hindu teacher, much respected and now deceased, who recognized the truth of essence and formulated his method according to the essential aspect of self is Ramana Maharshi:

> When the mind in the form of the ego, which takes the body for the Self and strays outwards, is curbed within the Heart the sense of "I" in the body is relinquished, and inquiry made with a still mind as to who it is that dwells in the body, a subtle illumination will be experienced as "I— I", which is no other than the Absolute, the Self, seated in the lotus of the Heart, in the city of the body, the tabernacle of God.[27]

> "Who am I?" I am not this physical body, nor am I the fine organs of sense perception; I am not the fine organs of external activity, nor am I the fine vital forces, nor am I even the thinking mind. Neither am I that unconscious state of nescience which retains merely the subtle vasanas (latencies of the mind), which being free from the functional activity of the sense-organs and of the mind, and being unaware of the existence of the objects of sense perception.
>
> Therefore, summarily rejecting all the above mentioned physical adjuncts and their functions, saying "I am not this; no, nor am I this, nor this"—that which remains separate and alone by itself, that pure Awareness is what I am. This Awareness is by its very nature Sat-Chit-Ananda (Existence—Consciousness—Bliss).[28]

Another Indian teacher, Baba Muktananda, a contemporary guru, talks about his particular experience of realization as the experience of the blue pearl. He does not emphasize the substantial aspect of essence. He speaks of it as consciousness, although he connects consciousness to the experience of substance in some of his experiences. In the following he writes about the development of his experience of the blue pearl:

---

[27] Arthur Osborn, *The Collected Works of Ramana Maharshi* (York Beach, ME: Samuel Weiser, 1970), 29.
[28] Arthur Osborn, *The Collected Works of Ramana Maharshi*, 39–40.

The Blue Pearl, that had enlarged into a human form through an oval shape, stood before me. Its radiance began to wane. Then I discovered a blue human figure within it. How enchantingly beautiful! His blue form shimmered and sparkled! His body was not a product of human fluids, the seven components. Nay, it was composed of the blue rays of Consciousness which, according to Tukaram Maharaj, condense into the eye lotion that grants divine vision. He was a mass of pure Awareness, the Life of Muktananda's inner life.[29]

Muktananda in his concern with the blue is focusing on consciousness. Consciousness is an aspect of essence, or in other words, the blue is the essence in the aspect of consciousness. Consciousness is a substance, although not as dense or substantial as will or love. The substance of consciousness is the substance of light. Seeing consciousness is like seeing the actual photons that constitute the inner light.

The "eye lotion" that he describes in the above passage is the condensation of the rays of consciousness, the condensed consciousness that Aurobindo called the force and we call the essence. To show the substantiality of the essential aspect that Muktananda calls the blue pearl and the substantial quality of his other experiences we cite more passages from his autobiographical book:

In meditation, I beheld the rare Blue Pearl, ambrosial and radiant, in manifold variations. . . .

As meditation in the sahasrar becomes stabilized, accompanied by rolls of thunder therein, the tongue curls upward into the nasopharynx and remains there. As a result, the seeker begins to sip heavenly juice. Sometimes, while the tongue is in this position, the cool dew of the moon is released. As he enjoys it, he is filled with wonderment. He practices sadhana with greater zeal in order to drink more of the nectar. There are many varieties of this fluid, tasting like butter, milk, ghee, buttermilk, and honey. This flow begins when the seeker's mind is merged in the ajna Chak-

---

[29] Swami Muktananda, *Guru* (New York: Harper & Row, 1971), 153.

ra and he perceives his own soul as the wickless flame shining in the space between the eye brows. It destroys many internal diseases. . . .

After the vision of the Blue Person, my mind would converge on the upper akasha in meditation, where I discerned glowing vapors enfolding the Blue Pearl in their center. This brightness intensified each day. It is said that the radiance of sahasrar is derived from the Blue Pearl. Each time in meditation, the awareness, "I am the Soul," arose. Sometimes I found that the Blue Pearl kept moving in and out of sahasrar for a short while.[30]

Muktananda is one of the rare teachers who specifically describes how certain essential aspects are experienced and seen. He mentions the blue pearl; as we see, he understands it as his own nature and presence. Muktananda emphasized his own experience, which is of the blue pearl, and does not mention that the pearl stands for a certain essential realm or dimension that has a particular significance. He does not mention that essence can manifest as pearls of different colors, each color having a particular meaning. For instance, blue is the color of consciousness, gold is the color of love, or merging love, as we have already mentioned, and so on for other colors.

In Buddhism, the understanding of essence and its substantiality is completely ignored until one reaches the levels of the *tantras*, the realm of the Tibetan Vajrayana Buddhism. Before that, in the realms of the Theravada (Hinayana) and the Mahayana, the emphasis is on the dissolution of the ego and the resulting experience of emptiness. Even in the tantras, the substantiality of essence is not directly emphasized, although it is understood and even used in practices.

From the perspective of the tantras, essence is looked at as subtle consciousness. The subtle consciousness is considered to be what realizes emptiness, but sometimes it is also seen as emptiness itself. The substantiality of this subtle consciousness is attested to by describing it as inner air, just as Idries Shah did in a previous passage. Here, the Dalai Lama talks about this consciousness:

---

[30] Swami Muktananda, *Guru*, 156–158.

Consciousness alone can apprehend the past events. It must be with the subtle consciousness. For example, when the subtle mind of clear light manifests at death, the brain is already finished. From the point of view of its cognition, it's called consciousness, and from the point of view of its engaging, or moving to its object, it's called inner air or energy. The very subtle air and consciousness are one undifferentiable entity. They are one entity differentiated only for thought or by way of their opposites.[31]

This aspect of essence, which the Dalai Lama calls subtle consciousness, subtle air, subtle energy, subtle mind, subtle body, and clear light is an aspect of essence connected with the state of awakening. We call it clear essence or the awake essence. This quality of clarity and awakeness is characteristic of Buddhism in general. This is contrasted with the blue consciousness of Muktananda, which is more characteristic of samadhi or absorption. This shows the main difference of emphasis between Buddhism and Hinduism: Buddhism emphasizes awakening, and Hinduism emphasizes samadhi (absorption), as ways toward enlightenment. Both of these qualities are seen as consciousness because they are aspects of essence corresponding to the centers of the head. The heart centers will manifest essence in different aspects, which are those of love. Buddhism is aware of the heart qualities as essential substances. This knowledge is used in some of their tantric practices, as when they mention *amrita*, or nectar, the nectar of the gods.

In one of the songs of Milarepa, Tibet's great yogi, nectar is equated with blessing.

The gift of blessing is bestowed by the Dakinis;
The nectar of Samaya is abundant nourishment;
Through faithful devotion the organs of sense are fed.
Propitious merits are thus garnered by my disciples.[32]

---

[31] John F. Avedon, *Interview with the Dalai Lama*, 62.
[32] G. Chang, trans., *The Hundred Thousand Songs of Milarepa* (New York: Harper & Row, 1970), 17.

So the nectar, which is the essential substance, is recognized by Milarepa as a blessing that is a spiritual nourishment.

In *Tibetan Yoga*, Evans-Wentz describes many of the Tibetan Buddhist practices. In one of the practices, the yoga of non-ego, he describes how all manifestations are transmuted into *amrita*, the drink of the gods. After giving certain mantras, he gives the instructions to the yogin: "Repeat the above *mantras* several times and think that thereby the impurities [of the body offered in the mystic sacrifice] have been purged away and the offering as a whole hath been transmuted into the *amrita* and that the *amrita* has been enclosed into universe-filling quantities [for the good of all beings]."[33]

In another book, Evans-Wentz writes about *amrita* in the life of Tibet's great guru Padma-Sambhava: "The Buddha of Medicine appeared before Padma, and, giving to him a pot of amrita, requested him to drink of it. Padma drank one half of it for the prolongation of his life and the other half he hid in a stupa; and now he was called 'Padma the one of accomplishment.'"[34]

We see here that the *amrita* or nectar, which is obviously some kind of nonphysical substance, is considered the spiritual nourishment needed for the realization of enlightenment.

A large part of Tibetan Buddhism is formulated in an alchemical language, indicating that it deals with subtle substances. The word for essential substance, *bodhi-citta*, is translated sometimes as the elixir of enlightenment and sometimes as the mind of enlightenment, or the thought of enlightenment. Although Buddhism does not single out the substantial nature of bodhi-citta, it is usually described as a substance with physical characteristics. The following passage, describing the final phase of the famous yoga of the inner fire (Tum-mo), illustrates the substantial nature of bodhi-citta:

> This is demonstrated by the notion that in the moment in which the "A" and the "HAM" unite in the word-symbol "AHAM," it dissolves; because in the heat of the flaming

---

[33] W. Y. Evans-Wentz, *Tibetan Yoga and Secret Doctrines* (Oxford: Oxford University Press, 1935), 312.

[34] W. Y. Evans-Wentz, ed., *The Tibetan Book of the Great Liberation* (Oxford: Oxford University Press, 1954), 138.

"A" the "HAM" is melted and flows down as the Elixir of Enlightenment (skt: bodhi-citta; Tib: byan-chub-sems) into all psychic centers of the body, "until not even the smallest part of it remains unpervaded."[35]

This practice is specifically for the realization of the essential substance. The substantiality of bodhi-citta is not emphasized, probably so as not to encourage attachment, which would inhibit the movement to enlightenment. Although enlightenment is not only the perception of essence, freedom from the narrowness and fixation of the personality—bodhi-citta, essence—is seen as what leads to this freedom. Bodhi-citta is called the elixir of enlightenment because it is recognized to be the agent of transformation, the alchemical agent needed to catalyze the process of transformation.

Therefore it is said in the Santideva's immortal work, "The Path towards Enlightenment" (Bodhicaryavatra):

He who wants to avoid the hundredfold pain of existence,
who wants to still the sufferings of sentient beings,
who wants to enjoy the hundredfold happiness (of the spirit),
such a one must never abandon the Thought of Enlightenment.

As soon as the Thought of Enlightenment takes root in him,
the miserable one who is fettered by passions to the prison
of existence, becomes immediately a son of the Buddhas.
He becomes worthy of veneration in the world of men and of gods.

As soon as this thought has taken possession of this unclean body

---

[35] Lama Anagarika Govinda, *Foundations of Tibetan Mysticism* (York Beach, ME: Samuel Weiser, 1969; and London: Rider & Co. 1960), 171. This and subsequent references used by permission.

it transforms it into the precious gem of a Buddha's
   body.
Therefore, take hold of this elixir, which causes this
   wonderful transformation,
and which is called the Thought of Enlightenment.[36]

Describing the symbols of alchemy, Lama Govinda writes:

The "Philosopher's Stone" is one of these invisible symbols,
and perhaps one of the most interesting and mysterious,
because it has given rise to many visible symbols, great
thoughts and discoveries in the realms of philosophy and
science. The eternal vision behind it, is that of the prima
materia, the original substance, the ultimate principle of
the world. According to this idea, all existing elements or
phenomena are only variations of the same force or substance, which can be restored to its purity by reducing and
dissolving the manifold qualities which have imposed
themselves upon it through differentiation and subsequent
specialization. Therefore, he who succeeds in penetrating
to the purity of its undifferentiated primordial form, has
gained the key to the secret of all creative power, which is
based on the mutability of all elements and phenomena.[37]

Writing about the pure consciousness that Buddha said exists in the
state of enlightenment, he says:

He who realized this, has truly found the philosopher's
stone, the precious jewel (mani), the prima materia of the
human mind, nay, of the very faculty of consciousness in
whatever form of life it might appear. This was the real aim
of all great alchemists, who knew that "mercury" stood for
the creative forces of higher consciousness, which had to be
freed from the gross elements of matter in order to attain
the state of perfect purity and radiance, the state of
Enlightenment.[38]

---

[36] Lama Anagarika Govinda, *Foundations of Tibetan Mysticism*, 273–274.

[37] Lama Anagarika Govinda, *Foundations of Tibetan Mysticism*, 51.

[38] Lama Anagarika Govinda, *Foundations of Tibetan Mysticism*, 59.

Discussing the philosopher's stone of Buddhism as *mani*, he writes:

> He who possesses this shining jewel overcomes death and rebirth, and gains immortality and liberation. But this jewel cannot be found anywhere except in the lotus (padma) of one's own heart.

Here mani is indeed the philosopher's stone, the cintamani, the wish-granting jewel of innumerable Buddhist legends, which in Tibet until the present day stands in the centre of folklore and religious poetry.

In later forms of Buddhism the idea of the jewel took the form of the Diamond Sceptre, the Vajra, and became as such the most important symbol for the transcendental qualities of Buddhism.

* * *

The vajra is regarded as the symbol of highest spiritual power which is irresistible and invincible. It is therefore compared to the diamond, which is capable of cutting asunder any other substance; but which itself cannot be cut by anything.

Likewise the properties of preciousness—nay, of supreme value—of changelessness, purity and clarity, were further reasons why in Buddhism the vajra was equated with the diamond. This is expressed in such terms as "Diamond Throne" (vajrasana), for the place on which the Buddha attained enlightenment, "Diamond Saw" (vajracchedika) for one of the most profound philosophical scriptures of the Mahayana, which ends with the words: "This sacred exposition shall be known as Vajracchedika-prajna-paramita-sutra—because it is hard and sharp like a diamond, cutting off all arbitrary conceptions and leading to the other shore of "Enlightenment."

The schools of Buddhism which placed this teaching in the centre of their religious life and thought are therefore known under the collective term "Vajrayana," the Diamond Vehicle.[39]

We see here Lama Govinda speaking of essence, the *prima materia*, in terms of the elixir of life, or the philosopher's stone of alchemy. He

---

[39] Lama Anagarika Govinda, *Foundations of Tibetan Mysticism*, 61–62.

refers to the *vajra*, the wish-fulfilling gem, as what leads to enlightenment. He writes of these phenomena as symbols and considers their properties as hardness, clarity, sharpness, and so on. He does not mention their most obvious and most fundamental property, which is substantiality. If the vajra (diamond) is a symbol, then is Muktananda's blue pearl a symbol? The deep truth of substantiality is kept secret, yet the terms plainly describe what is experienced.

We notice again the Buddhist emphasis on the diamond, instead of the pearl, in contrast to Muktananda. The diamond (vajra) is another dimension of essence, just as the pearl is a dimension of essence. It reflects the Buddhist emphasis on the mind. It is the essence in the objective, impersonal aspects, whereas the pearl expresses the essence in its personal (in contrast to impersonal) aspects. This is another of the main differences between Buddhism and Hinduism.

We see here the real meaning of alchemy. Alchemy is usually considered a mysterious science, full of symbols, secret processes, and esoteric terms. Many believe that the alchemical terminology is a symbolic representation of inner events and processes. This is partially true. It is true that the terminology refers to inner processes, but it is not true that the language is symbolic. It appears symbolic only to one who does not know that essence is a subtle substance with physical characteristics. Alchemy refers to processes involving actual substances on the subtle or essential dimension and not on the corporeal level. Most of the terminology is really descriptive. The alchemists try to describe their work in terms that are most direct and literal. For outsiders, the terms can be understood only as symbolic of something else. Outsiders think that when alchemists use the term *sun*, they must be "referring to some kind of mental or spiritual process or perception." This is both true and untrue. It is true in that they are referring to essential perception. It is not true in that the alchemists actually mean sun—the physical sun in the sky— but a distinct essential reality that the word *sun* describes better than any other word. For the true alchemists, everything that exists in the physical universe has its inner counterpart, and the physical object is not necessarily taken to be more real than the inner one. This is expressed in the Emerald Tablet, ascribed to Hermes, the Father of Western alchemy, which says, "What is above is like what is below. What is below is like what is above."

The human organism is a miniature universe. This is true in so many ways that most people would be completely astounded if they were to see this reality for themselves. The outsider can think of alchemical language only as symbolic, because this is easier to accept than the actual truth of alchemy. So again, alchemy is hidden by its unlikelihood. It is hidden because its truth is unexpected. We are not trying to be mysterious. We are stating the obvious facts in plain language. There are some complications in the matter of alchemical texts because some authors do not really understand the quintessence of alchemy, or they understand it only partially. Some alchemists used some terms symbolically, whereas more knowledgeable ones knew they were not symbolic but literal or parallel. This makes most books about alchemy full of contradictions, which in turn makes it almost useless, if not completely misleading, for most people to read alchemical texts. The individual has to be steeped in the direct knowledge of essential development in order to understand alchemical texts and to see that alchemy is literally the science of inner chemistry, or the science dealing with subtle substances. We can see this more clearly in Eastern books of alchemy, as in the passage we quote below from a Taoist text on alchemy. As we read this text we see that subtle energies are used to produce the elixir, the golden nectar. We also learn that the Taoists know about the pearl aspect of essence:

> When the breath remains (nearly) stationary, the (immortal) foetus will be as secure as a mountain and by continuing his practice he will achieve minor and major serenity; all phenomena will be absorbed into nothingness and with spirit frozen in this state by day and night, the bright pearl will form in this unperturbed nothingness. If this serenity is not achieved the immortal seed cannot be produced. The moment when he enters this serenity is likened to his approaching death that precedes the resurrection which is the main object of alchemy. As to how death is followed by resurrection, this concerns the method of producing the bright pearl.[40]

We notice first that the pearl is not described as blue, the way Muktananda does, indicating that the pearl can have other colors. We also see here the pearl considered in relation to resurrection or

---

[40] Charles Luk, *Taoist Yoga* (York Beach, ME: Samuel Weiser, 1970), 96.

rebirth. This theme of the pearl as the resurrection body appears in some Sufi writings. We quote a passage from Shaikh Ahmad Ahsai of the nineteenth century to illustrate the fact that alchemy is the science of subtle substances.

> For, in the last analysis, spirits are light—being in the fluid state (nur wujudi dhaib). Bodies are also light—being, but in the solid state. The difference between them is the same as the difference between water and snow. This is why the evidence tending to the affirmation of the "return" of spirits is itself the evidence tending to affirm the resurrection of bodies. . . .
>
> The alchemical Work testifies to the validity of this affirmation. The fact is that bodies that have reached maturity and completeness through this operation are in the liquid-solid state. This is what the First Imam, Ali ibn Ali-Talib, declares according to the report of his biographer Ibn Shahr-Ashub, and of Abul-Abbas in his book bringing to light the secret concerning the science of the Elixir. Someone therefore asked the Imam about alchemy, when he was delivering a discourse: "It is the sister of prophecy," he explained: "for there is an immunity which keeps prophecy from being desecrated, which is that ordinary people do no more than discuss its literal outer meaning. I call God to witness that it is none other than water in the solid state, immobilized air, compact fire, fluid earth. For earth in the fluid state is water in the solid state. In the same sense bodies also are spirits. . . .

☩ ☩ ☩

> Mulla Sadra Shirazi: "The soul is spiritual 'matter' (madda ruhaniya), a subtle organism that can only receive Forms which are themselves in the subtle and suprasensory state, such that they are not perceptible to the physical senses, but only to the organs of psycho-spiritual perception (the suprasensory senses.)"[41]

---

[41] Henry Corbin, *Spiritual Body and Celestial Earth*, trans. Nancy Pearson, Bollingen Series 91, Vol. 2. Copyright © 1977 by Princeton University Press, Excerpts, pp. 205–206.

Although it is clear that in texts like these references to substances are not symbolic, modern authors continue to take the symbolic meaning. This is of course a reflection of the fact that these authors are bound by their minds; they cannot see that essence is something more fundamental and more substantial than the mind and its manifestations. They remain on the mental realm of symbols and images and shy away from the embodied experience of being. A well-known example is that of the psychologist Carl Jung and his followers. He understood alchemical language to be symbolic of mental and psychic processes. He took the terms *water of life, the philosopher's stone, Mercurius*, and many others as symbols and metaphors of psychic and spiritual processes. In this way he got closer to the truth than those people who totally dismiss alchemy, but he fell short of the truth of alchemy. He could not go beyond his mind and his intuition, and so his development could not go to essential realization. His psychology stayed on the level of the mind, and his archetypes remained as disembodied images. He saw the soul as containing images, instead of actual presence, as the following passage indicates:

> I can only stand in deepest awe and admiration before the depths and heights of the soul whose world beyond space hides an immeasurable richness of images, which millions of years of living have stored up and condensed into organic material. My conscious mind is like an eye which perceives the furthermost spaces; but the psychic non-ego is that which fills this space in a sense beyond space. These images are not pale shadows, but powerful and effective conditions of the soul which we can only misunderstand but can never rob of their power by denying them.[42]

Ira Progoff, a student of Jung, writes about Jung's conception of the self archetype:

> The important point is that as a proto-image the Self represents a reality that is an actual possibility for the human organism, and it heretofore is intimately involved

---

[42] C. G. Jung, *Psychological Reflections* (New York: Harper & Row, 1957), 38.

in all the stages of man's psychological development. The archetype of the Self is expressed in the form of many historical symbols that represent various phases of the individuation process in the life history of nations. A particularly frequent symbol of the Self is the "Divine Child," which often appears also as a savior-messiah. In alchemical types of symbolism the Self as the ultimate achievement of psychological work is represented as "the pearl of great worth," the "philosopher's stone," or other symbols that convey the emergence of a small precious jewel as the result of integration of the psyche.[43]

In the passages quoted above from Indian, Taoist, Hindu, and Sufi sources, the pearl, the gem, and the like are not symbols and not images. They are actual presences of essence in various aspects. "Jung's personal experience of the Self is, in other words, as a symbol that represents the reality of life."[44] However, when a realized person uses the terms *pearl, diamond body,* and so on, they mean the reality of their inner life and not symbols representing it.

Carl Jung had a very broad and deep understanding, but he remained on the level of psychology, although he attempted to understand essential experiences. Because of this, his psychology can be of much greater use if we add to it the knowledge that inner essential development deals with subtle substances, not just with psychic images. We can see then that the images are only the vague products of the essential experiences, on the level of the mind. We can see that the archetype of the self, for instance, is not an archetypal image but a substantial ontological presence that has infinitely more significance than any image.

It is easy for one who understands essence to see which of Jung's archetypes are faithful representations of essential aspects, which ones are distorted, and how much they are distorted from the actual objective "seeing" of the essence. We believe this to be a worthy and useful endeavor and hope that somebody with the necessary knowledge will undertake it.

---

[43] Reprinted from *The Death and Rebirth of Psychology* by Ira Progoff, p. 182. Copyright © 1956 by Ira Progoff. Used by permission of Julian Press, Inc.

[44] Ira Progoff, *The Death and Rebirth of Psychology,* 187.

For instance, we have already mentioned the essential aspect of the diamond body and related it to the archetype of the wise old man. The archetype tells us it is the part of our collective unconscious that functions as a guide for inner development. This is true of the diamond body, and hence the archetypal image is useful here. However, if we stay on the level of the image, we will not come to the diamond body; we will miss seeing that it is a guide because it is pure objective knowledge. Thus, we will not have complete and permanent access to this guide and its knowledge.

ESSENCE

We have asserted the truth of substantiality to impress on the reader that essence or being is not a state of mind but is an actual and palpable ontological presence. The substantiality of essence is a fact that must be taken into consideration for the process of development, but simply realizing this truth is not sufficient. This is because, for instance, the physical body is also a substantial presence. We have stated and asserted the truth of substantiality to impress on the reader that essence or being is not an insight, not a state of mind, but an actual and palpable ontological presence.

So what differentiates essential substance from the other categories of experience? In Chapter One we discussed essence from the perspective of presence and from the deeper perspective of existence. Essence and existence are the same thing. The essential substance is experienced in its deepest nature as existence. This level of experience is so deep and profound, so full and packed with a live significance, so moving and so powerful that it is not possible to communicate it through words. Words can describe some aspects of experience, but they fail actually to deliver the whole impact. Words can communicate the experience to somebody who already has had it or is right on the verge of it, but not to somebody who does not know.

The usual contention in spiritual literature, that being cannot be talked about or described, is not quite accurate. Essence can be described, just like anything else, with words and images. This does not mean that someone who hasn't had the experience will understand the description. However, one who has had the experience will easily understand what the description is referring to. But this is true for anything, not just essence. If somebody has never seen or eaten a persimmon, he will not be able to understand a description of a persimmon; but on hearing a description, he will likely envision something else, familiar from his past experience.

The same holds true for descriptions of essence. The difficulty is not in describing it in words but in making sense to someone who does not have the experience. The person will be able to understand the words but will be incapable of connecting the description to his experience. He will construct something in his mind that will correspond to the description. This construction will be false because he lacks the actual experience. However, as in the analogy above, a person who has seen or eaten a persimmon will understand the description right away. So when I say "existence," a person who has had the experience of existence will understand. The person who has not will either see that he does not understand or will take something else in his experience to mean existence.

So the difficulty with language in terms of essence is not in describing it but in communicating it. This is important to understand, so that the interested person will not be oriented toward something vague, general, imprecise, and inaccessible. The experience of essence is very clear, very precise, and very definite. In fact, it is much more definite and precise an experience than that of a thought or an emotion.

Of course, language cannot capture everything about essence. We cannot describe essence in all of its characteristics and nuances. But its experience can be communicated to somebody who is familiar with it or close to the experience. This is true about any category of experience. For instance, we cannot completely describe heat, but we can describe it enough to be able to communicate to somebody who knows about heat.

"From such experiences we begin to understand the significance of the deep blue as the centre and starting-point of meditative symbolism and vision: it is the light of the transcendental Wisdom of the Dharma-dhatu—the origin of the very faculty of consciousness and knowledge, undifferentiated, potential, all-embracing like infinite space."[45] It is not possible to describe such an experience in its fullness, but it can be pointed to, as in this passage by Lama Govinda, for someone who knows the experience.

---

[45] Lama Anagarika Govinda, *Foundations of Tibetan Mysticism*, 117.

There are certain modes of experiencing essence in which it becomes difficult to describe the experience. It depends on what kind of perceptual relation we have with essence. In certain experiences, especially in those that do not involve the presence of the discriminating consciousness, description becomes impossible because there is no conceptual activity going on. There is no description because there are no concepts, and concepts are needed for verbal communication. Certain aspects of essence have this effect on the usual consciousness; some aspects eliminate the discriminating consciousness. All differentiating concepts are annihilated.

But we must use concepts if we are going to communicate verbally. One important concept that we have been using without clarification is that of essential aspects—that essence has many aspects, not just one quality. As we have seen, essential substance has precise and definite physical characteristics. In fact, it can be described in terms of color, taste, texture, transparency, density, luminosity, viscosity, and so on. Variations in these give rise to different aspects of essence, which have different psychological significance.

So although essence is one, the same substance, it has many varieties, many qualities. These are aspects of essence. This is true for both the baby and the adult. The aspect of truth is not the same as the aspect of love, and this is not the same as the aspect of will, and so on. They are all essence, and clearly so for the one who knows, but they are experienced differently and affect us differently.

This fact is not stressed by most systems of inner development because it is not used much by these systems. One reason for this is that some of these systems base their method on the contrast between essence and personality, and the work is then to free the essence as a whole from the personality as a whole. Another reason is that some systems do not pay attention to essence at all; they look at the personality, see it as the barrier to freedom and the cause of suffering, and work on dissolving its narrowness. Still another reason is that some systems are based on only one aspect of essence, which is emphasized and seen as the real truth or the only reality, ignoring other aspects.

The lack of stress on the variety of essential aspects is sometimes more apparent than real. This fact is important only for the students who are advanced in their training, the ones who are involved in an intimate way with a school or teacher, receiving the oral teaching.

However, some systems do acknowledge the existence of the various absolute aspects of essence, and this fact is then used in the methods of teaching. The Sufis, in fact, look at essence or the soul as having different modes of existence: "As for the doctrinal aspects of Sufi psychology, the human soul is then presented as a substance that possesses different faculties and modes of existence, separated yet united by a single axis that transverses all the modes and planes."[46]

This fact is used in Sufi methodology in the concept of "stations," which are stages of inner development. This development is seen as a transformation of essential substance from one aspect to another, until they are all realized. Essential transformation is, in other words, transubstantiation: "A state or station, like patience (sabr) or confidence (tamabkul), is a virtue, which means that when the soul reaches such a state not only does it possess the virtue in question as one accident, but its very substance is transformed by it so that during that stage of the Way in a sense it is itself that virtue."[47]

In Buddhism, the Tibetan Vajrayana schools acknowledge and use this fact, for instance, in their concept of the Buddha families, called the "Dhyani-Buddhas":

> The forms in which the Dhyani-Buddhas appear in the creative phase of inner vision in the process of meditation, have been compared by us with the different colors into which the rays of the sun are separated, when passing through a prism, thus revealing in each color a particular quality of light. This comparison is all the more adequate, as colors play an important role in the appearances of the Dhyani-Buddhas. Their colors indicate certain properties and spiritual associations, which to the initiate are as significant and meaningful as notes to the musically trained. They convey the particular vibration characteristic for each aspect of transcendental knowledge or Wisdom, which in the realm of sound is expressed by the corresponding vibration of the mantra, in the realm of corporeality by the corresponding gesture or mudra, and in the innermost realm by the corresponding spiritual attitude.[48]

---

[46] Seyyed Hassein Nasr, *Sufi Essays* (New York: Schocken Books, 1977), 47.

[47] Seyyed Hassein Nasr, *Sufi Essays*, 70.

[48] Lama Anagarika Govinda, *Foundations of Tibetan Mysticism*, 115.

Other systems, for instance those originating from the Judeo-Christian traditions, use the idea of angels to denote essential aspects. Other systems, like Zoroastrianism, made this the most important feature of their world view: "Angelology is one of the characteristic features of Zoroastrian Mazdaism, for which reason it can neither be reduced to an abstract and monolithic type of monotheism, nor invalidated by what people have tried to interpret as a return to the "ancient gods," or a restoration of pre-Zoroastrian polytheism."[49]

These essential aspects are absolute in the sense that they cannot be reduced to anything else. Truth is always truth and always feels the same. In other words, regardless of how much the person changes, truth still retains its specific substantial characteristics. This permanently absolute aspect of truth remains the same for every human being. Whenever it is experienced by anyone, it is experienced as the same thing. It is universal truth. In other words, its substantial characteristics of texture, taste, color, density, and so on are invariant for everybody. As we have stressed before, essence is an objective ontological presence, which means that the personal subjectivity does not touch it.

This understanding of the existence of essence in different and various aspects will be useful later on for understanding how it is lost and how it can be regained. We will content ourselves here with an attempt to communicate its most basic and general characteristics.

It is true that essence is a substance, but it is not an inert substance. It is a substance that in itself is life, awareness, existence. Take clear water, for example. Imagine that this water is self-aware, that each molecule is aware of itself and of its own energy and excitation. Imagine now that you are this aware substance, the water. This is close to an experience of essential substance. Of course, this is hard to imagine for someone who does not know essence. And the essential experience is much more than this. Essence is not alive; it *is* aliveness. It is not aware; it *is* awareness. It does not have the quality of existence; it *is* existence. It is not loving; it *is* love. It is not joyful; it *is* joy. It is not true; it *is* truth.

The quality of aliveness of essence is of a different order from that of the body. The body is alive, but essence is life itself. Essence is

---

[49] Henry Corbin, *Spiritual Body and Celestial Earth*, 5.

like packed, condensed, concentrated, completely pure life. It is 100 percent life. It is like a substance in which each atom is packed with live existence. Here, life and existence are not concepts, not ideas or abstract descriptions; rather, they are the most alive, most intimate, richest, deepest, most moving, and most touching stirrings within us. The experience of essential substance can have such a depth, such a richness, such a realness, such a meaningfulness, and such an impact on our minds that some people actually get dizzy, unable to take the impact directly.

It is not experienced as something alien, distant, or neutral, like a physical object or an idea. No, we experience it as that which is most intimately ourselves. It is most deeply our nature, and it is the most precious and most beautiful center of us. It is our significance, our meaning, our nature, our identity. It is what moves our hearts, illuminates our minds, fulfills our lives. It is so near a thing to our hearts that only the heart can taste it. It is so near a thing to us that it is actually the very substance of our identity. It is so significant a thing for us that it is the only true nutrient for our life. It is the reality of us, the truth of us. It is the very substance of truth and the innermost secret of all truths. It is the most precious thing in existence.

Essential substance is so beautiful and magnificent that no imagination can conceive of its beauty, and no poetry can convey its magnificence. The way it moves us and teaches us is beyond the wildest dreams and imaginations of humanity. Its potentialities are staggering, its creativity is boundless, its depth is endless, and its intelligence is limitless. It is a wonder—a wonder beyond all miracles. It is our true nature, our most intimate identity.

This wonder is not just for stories or poetry. It is not just to dream about or long for. It is not just to give us flashes of its magnificence, or fleeting tastes of its significance. It is actually our human essence. It is who we are: our very beingness. We are to be this essence, to exist and live as essence. It is our potential to be our essence, not just in occasional experiences but always and permanently. It is our essence that can and should be what lives, and what should be the center of our life. It can and should be inseparable from us. The work of inner development is not aimed only at having an experience of essence. It is aimed at the complete realization of essence and the permanent existence of us as essence. It is aimed at the eradication of our separation from essence. To be free is simply to be. And to be is simply to live as essence. In fact, when we are not consciously essence, we are not existing. The life of the personality is nonexistence, a wasted and useless life. There is life only when there is existence, and existence is essence.

To be a genuine human being, a complete human being, is to be essence. To be essence is then not just an inner experience, but a total experience—a complete life. Life is then the life of essence, both inner and outer, in the privacy of our hearts and in the shared experience with others. Essence is then what dictates our actions, what determines our way of life, and what shapes our environment. This is real harmony.

CHAPTER THREE

THE LOSS OF ESSENCE

F ESSENCE IS WHO WE ARE, our true nature, then why is the majority of humanity not in touch with it at all? Why is it something we seek? To answer this question it is useful to observe young children and babies, from the perspective of essence. The many studies of children and babies made by psychologists in the past few decades have developed much useful knowledge. Of course, these studies have not been from the perspective of essence but from social, psychological, or physiological perspectives. They are usually conducted by researchers whose world views do not include essence. But now we need information about essence and young children. We can obtain this information by observing not only with our two eyes but with the subtle capacities of perception, the subtle organs of perception that can be aware of essence directly, without any inference. This is the only way essence can be observed and studied. Then we need to compare these observations with those of adults.

What we find when we observe in this way is that babies and very young children not only have essence, they are in touch with their essence; they are identified with their essence; they are the essence. The inner experience of a baby is mostly of the essence in its various qualities. This does not mean that the baby is conceptually aware of the existence of essence. The baby knows essence very well, and very intimately, but without mental involvement and without cognition. We know this from the experience of adults who discover their essence and remember knowing it, in some fashion, from their childhood. In other words, the baby knows essence but does not know that he knows. He is not awake to its presence and its nature.

The fact that human beings are born with essence has been known from ancient times. The baby is not only born with essence, but essence is the baby that is born. In describing essence, Gurdjieff says: "It must be understood that man consists of two parts: essence and personality. Essence in man is what is his own. Personality in man is what is 'not his own.' A small child has no personality as yet. He is what he really is. He is essence. His desires, tastes, likes, dislikes, express his being such as it is."[1]

So we can conclude that people are born with essence but end up without it later on. Obviously, it is somehow lost, or the connection with it is lost. This does not mean that a baby experiences essence exactly the way an adult does. A baby does experience essence, but for the adult it will be more developed, more expanded, more distinct, more powerful, and it will function in ways that are only a potential in a baby. The baby's essence does not have the immensity, the depth, and the richness of the adult's experience of essence. It is generally lighter, in a sense, more diluted. The adult can experience his essence in such a light and fluffy mode, but it has more dimension and significance. Its capacities are more grown and developed. An adult also has the possibility of awakening to the presence of essence and its nature.

It would be interesting to observe the development of essence from babyhood to adulthood without interruption or loss. This would mean observing a person who does not lose his essence or the connection to it. But this possibility is so rare and unlikely that for all practical purposes it is nonexistent. We can, however, observe what happens to the human being's essence under normal circumstances, from babyhood to adulthood. What we see is a gradual loss of essence.

---

[1] P. D. Ouspensky, *In Search of the Miraculous* (New York: Harcourt, Brace & World, 1949), 232. Used by permission.

The fact of loss of essence also has been known from ancient times, at least by some. The human being is born with essence, but essence is lost after a while, and by adulthood the person is just vaguely aware of some lack or incompleteness. That is why the process of discovery and inner development is often seen as a process of return or remembering. Many teaching stories depict the loss and retrieval of essence. One such story, "Hymn of the Soul," tells the sequence in beautiful and graphic detail:

> When I was an infant child in a palace of my Father and resting in the wealth and luxury of my nurturers, out of the East, our native country, my parents provisioned me and sent me, and of the wealth of those their treasures they put together a load, both great and light, that I might carry it alone. . . .
>
> And they armed me with adamant, which breaketh iron, and they took off from me the garment set with gems, spangled with gold, which they had made for me because they loved me, and the robe was yellow in hue, made for my stature.
>
> And they made a covenant with me and inscribed it on mine understanding, that I should not forget it, and said: If thou go down into Egypt and bring back thence the one pearl which is there in the midst of the sea girt about by the devouring serpent, thou shalt again put on the garment set with gems and the robe whereupon it resteth and become with thy brother that is next unto us an heir in our kingdom.
>
> And I came out of the East by a road difficult and fearful with two guides and I was untried in travelling by it. . . .
>
> But when I entered into Egypt, the guides left me which had journeyed with me.
>
> And I set forth by the quickest way to the serpent and by his hole I abode, watching for him to slumber and sleep that I might take my pearl from him. . . .
>
> And I put on the raiment of the Egyptians, lest I should seem strange, as one that had come from without to recover the pearl; and lest they should awake the serpent against me.

But I know not by what occasion they learned that I was not of their country, and with guile they mingled for me a deceit and I tasted of their food, and I knew no more that I was a king's son and I became a servant unto their king.

And I forgot also the pearl, for which my fathers had sent me, and by means of the heaviness of their food I fell into a deep sleep.

But when this befell me, my fathers also were aware of it and grieved for me, and a proclamation was published in our kingdom, that all should meet at our doors.

And then the kings of Parthia and they that bare office and the great ones of the East made a resolve concerning me, that I should not be left in Egypt, and the princes wrote unto me signifying thus:

From thy Father the King of kings, and thy mother that ruleth the East, and thy brother that is second unto us; unto our son that is in Egypt, peace. Rise up and awake out of sleep and hearken unto the words of the letter and remember that thou art a son of kings; lo, thou has come under the yoke of bondage. Remember the pearl for which thou wast sent into Egypt. Remember thy garment spangled with gold and the glorious mantle which thou shouldest wear and wherewith thou shouldest deck thyself. Thy name is in the book of life, and with thy brother thou shalt be in our kingdom. . . .

The letter flew and lighted down by me and became all speech, and I at the voice of it and the feeling of it started up out of sleep and I took it up and kissed and read it.

And it was written concerning that which was recorded in my heart, and I remembered forthwith that I was a son of kings, and my freedom yearned after its kind.

I remembered also the pearl, for which I was sent down into Egypt, and I began with charms against the terrible serpent and I overcame him by naming the name of my Father upon him. . . .

And I caught away the pearl and turned back to bear it unto my fathers, and I stripped off the filthy garment and left it in their land, and directed my way forthwith to the light of my fatherland in the East.

And on the way I found my letter that had awakened me and it, like as it had taken a voice and raised me when I slept, so also guided me with the light that came from it.

For at times the royal garment of silk shone before my eyes and with its voice and its guidance it also encouraged me to speed and with love leading me and drawing me onward. . . .

And when I stretched forth and received it and adorned myself with the beauty of the colours thereof and in my royal robe excelling in beauty I arrayed myself wholly.

And when I had put it on, I was lifted up unto the place of peace and homage and I bowed my head and worshipped the brightness of the Father which had sent it unto me, for I had performed his commandments and he likewise that which he had promised.

And at the doors of his palace which was from the beginning I mingled among his nobles, and he rejoiced over me and received me with him into his palace, and all his servants do praise him with sweet voices. . . .[2]

However, this story and many like it look at the whole matter from a metaphysical or cosmological perspective, which explains what happens in general terms and gives a sense of the point of the whole thing. This particular story, for instance, answers the question of the "why" of the loss and retrieval of essence. Here we want to look at the loss from the phenomenological and psychological perspective, so that we can use the information to help us in the process of return or retrieval. If we understand how essence is lost, if we see it specifically and in detail, we will be able to see how to go back, how to retrace our steps, so to speak.

Essence is gradually lost or covered up (veiled from our perception) as the personality develops. We tend to identify more and more with the personality that develops in response to our environment. By the end we forget that we even had essence. We end with the experience that there is only our personality, and that we are that personality, as if it always had been thus.

---

[2] M. R. James, trans., *The Apocryphal New Testament* (Oxford: Oxford University Press, 1924). Used by permission.

This gives us the hint that in order to allow our essence to emerge again, we need to learn to disidentify from the personality and the sense of ego identity. This, in fact, is the main method that most systems of inner development employ. This disidentification, which can culminate in the experience technically termed *ego death*, is the main requirement necessary for the discovery of essence.

Now let's look at this process more closely and in more detail. It is true that essence is lost gradually as personality develops and grows. Our awareness of essence dims slowly over the span of a few years until there is no awareness of essence at all. This is looking at essence as one undifferentiated mass or whole, which is lost or becomes far away from our consciousness. This is true, generally speaking, but the picture looks different if we use better lenses and if we focus our inner microscopes more finely.

We see that a baby's essence has many qualities or aspects of essence, which we discussed in Chapter Two. A certain aspect dominates when the baby is resting, another when he is active, another when he is playful, and so on. There is an interplay, a dance, between the various aspects, depending on the situation, the activity, the time, and so on.

Not only does the baby experience a dance of many qualities and aspects, we observe that as the baby grows, different aspects of essence dominate in different periods of his development. The aspects of essence mostly manifested depend on the age of the baby or the particular developmental phase he is going through. The particular aspects of each phase or stage of development are organically interconnected with the processes of development specific to such stages. For instance, from two months to about a year the aspect of essence dominant has to do with a kind of melting sweet love and merging with the environment, especially with the mother. This coincides with the developmental phase that is termed the *symbiotic stage* by the ego psychologists, a stage when the baby is still unaware of differentiation between himself and his mother. Around seven months old, another more active, more outwardly expansive aspect, which has to do with essential strength, starts to dominate. After a while, the qualities of joy and will become dominant, as the toddler becomes more aware of his environment and starts exploring it with joy and a sense of power. Then the aspect of essential value assumes dominance for some time. In fact, we can see the stages of essential development in relation to the stages of the development of the ego.

The ego psychologists are aware of the development of strength, value, joy, and so on, but they are usually unaware that these are aspects of essence. They see them as emotional or affective experiences of the personality as it develops and attains a permanent structure. We will leave the subject of the specific and precise relationships between essential aspects and ego developmental stages to a future publication and will use here only the general idea of the relative dominance of particular aspects of essence during different stages of the development of the child.

Because essence has various aspects, and different aspects dominate at different times and have different functions, essence is lost aspect by aspect. It is true that essence as a whole is gradually lost as the personality develops, but we see within this overall process many specific processes, when various aspects of essence go through varying vicissitudes until they are finally lost. Each aspect has its own process and goes through its own vicissitudes, until it is finally buried. The total of all of these smaller processes make up the whole bigger process of the loss of essence. We observe that the aspect of love, for instance, goes through the vicissitudes of waxing and waning until it is finally dimmed and lost. And we see that this process is different from the processes that essential value, or will, or compassion, or emptiness go through. We see that certain aspects are lost before others. Some aspects are lost abruptly and some are lost gradually.

The point we want to make here, which no other system or tradition has emphasized, is that although essence as a whole goes through a process of dimming and eventual loss, specific essential aspects have different processes of development and varying vicissitudes. The environment affects essence as a whole, but it affects the different aspects differently. The aspect of the child's environment that finally shuts down the will might be different from the aspect that shuts down joy, for instance. This understanding of the loss of essence is of paramount importance when it comes to the question of techniques for retrieval of essence, as we will show in the next chapter.

Of course, ultimately, all aspects of essence must be veiled for some of them to be unconscious. If some aspects remain in the consciousness, they will tend to bring out other aspects spontaneously, except perhaps in instances of severe dissociation and splitting, which are the causes of severe mental pathologies. This is because

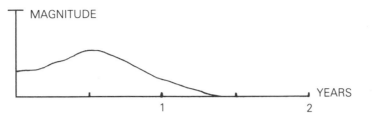

a) Merging essence will dominate between two months and ten months.

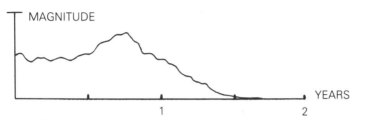

b) Strength will dominate approximately between six months and twelve months.

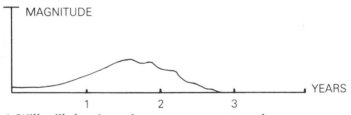

c) Will will dominate between one year and two years.

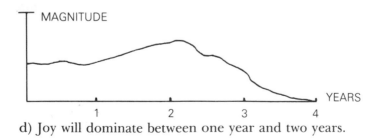

d) Joy will dominate between one year and two years.

Figure 1. a) The loss of essence over time is compared to the loss of b) strength, c) will, and d) joy.

essence has the characteristic of going deeper and opening whatever reality there is. If one aspect is present, without severe dissociation, it will naturally bring the rest of the aspects to consciousness.

We can understand the relation of the overall process of loss to the various smaller processes of specific losses by using a graph. Let's look at just a few aspects, for illustrative purposes—say, those of merging, strength, will, and joy. The graphs in Figure 1 will illustrate their specific processes. The vertical line denotes magnitude or intensity; the horizontal line denotes time, in years. If we put all the curves together to get the general overall curve, which is the summation of the four of them, we will get the process of the essence as a whole, as shown in Figure 2.

This perspective is not simply academic. It has far-reaching implications for the formulation of methods of retrieval and return to essence. First, we can see right away that what one person needs to do to return to essence is not necessarily the same as for another individual. It is true that everyone loses essence, but the processes of that dimming and loss are different for each person. Different aspects are more deeply buried in one person than in another. Thus, other aspects are closer to the surface in one individual than those

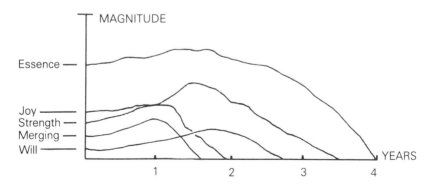

Figure 2. Here we see that the larger overall curve representing the vicissitudes of essence combines the various curves representing the different aspects. We need to remember that there are many other essential qualities not represented here, and that these curves vary from one individual to another; however, the variations will keep the general character of each curve.

same aspects in another. Obviously, the methods for the return to essence should be flexible enough to accommodate these individual differences. The amount of work that an individual needs to do to free a certain aspect might be different from that needed by another individual. The methods needed and the attitudes emphasized to free a certain aspect will be different from those needed for the other aspects of essence. The heart of the matter here is the possibility of specificity, precision, and flexibility in our methods and techniques.

We can look at the process of dimming and loss more closely, with better magnifying lenses. We have noted that essence is lost as the personality and its ego identity develop. We can understand this more specifically by looking at the vicissitudes of a specific essential aspect, as an example. Let's take the essential aspect of merging love. This aspect is present from the beginning of life but dominates especially between two and ten months of age. This period of life generally coincides with the period of ego development, called the symbiotic phase by Margaret Mahler:

> From the second month on, dim awareness of the need-satisfying object marks the beginning of the phase in which the infant behaves and functions as though he and his mother were an omnipotent system—a dual unity within one common boundary. . . .
>
> The term symbiosis in this context is a metaphor. Unlike the biological concept of symbiosis, it does not describe what actually happens in a mutually beneficial relationship between two separate individuals of different species. It describes that state of undifferentiation, of fusion with mother, in which the "I" is not yet differentiated from the "not-I" and in which inside and outside are only gradually coming to be seen as different.[3]

In this state of ego development, the child is not aware of the mother or himself as separate individuals in their own right. The ego has not separated out. Mother and self are still a unity—a dual unity. In infant observation, we find that when the infant experi-

---

[3] Margaret S. Mahler et al., *The Psychological Birth of the Human Infant* (New York: Basic Books, 1975), 44.

ences the dual unity without any frustration or conflict, his essential state is that of merging love. It is a pleasurable, sweet, melting kind of love. The baby is peaceful, happy, and contented.

However, as we have pointed out before, the baby is not aware of essence conceptually or from the perspective of an observer. He is the essence, so in this phase he experiences the dual unity of the symbiotic phase as the merging essence. What he is dimly aware of is the presence of mother and himself as "one," and this "one" is felt as merging love. As Mahler says, there is still no differentiation between inside and outside, between self and mother. It is a dual unity, and this is his perception. However, he is actually experiencing the merging aspect of essence. The child does not know that he is the merging love. There is still no sense of a separate self in this phase. So there is the impression, right at the beginning of the ego's formation, that the dual unity is merging essence. This initial and primitive impression of the baby is faulty because the merging essence is he himself. But we see that this wrong impression lies at the root of the personality. This equation of the dual unity with the merging essence remains in the unconscious, at the root of the personality, for the rest of the individual's life.

This is a subtle point but of fundamental importance in understanding the relation of the personality to essence. Whenever there is any loss of the symbiotic union, the dual unity with mother, the child experiences the loss of the merging essence. To repeat, this is because for him the merging love aspect of essence *is* he and his mother together. That is what he is aware of when there is merging love. He is not introspective, so he is not aware of the presence of this aspect of essence from an observer's point of view. He is enjoying the merging love but sees it as the undifferentiated union with mother. In his mind there develops, at the primitive level of his ego, the association of loving proximity with the mother to the merging love of essence.

Whenever this proximity, this symbiotic unity, is not there, the merging love of essence disappears. This satisfying symbiotic unity can be lost for many reasons: rejection by the mother, distance from her, frustration by her, too much clinging from her side, physical or emotional abandonment, actual loss, to mention a few.

This always happens because there is no perfect symbiotic relationship between mother and infant because of many factors, mostly unavoidable. However, the loss can occur in many different ways, some more painful than others, some sooner than others, some more abruptly than others, and so on. It would take us far away from our objective to go into the details here. We only need to know here that merging essence is at some point lost.

The baby experiences simultaneously the loss of the essential aspect of merging love and loss of the positive gratifying symbiotic relationship with the mother. He feels he lost the merging love, but he believes he lost the dual unity. He starts feeling incomplete because he lost an essential part of him, his merging love. He knows this only dimly, only subconsciously, so to speak. But what he observes is the loss of the gratifying symbiotic relationship with the mother, so naturally he assumes that his feeling of incompleteness is the result of the loss of this relationship. He in fact believes subconsciously, and in time unconsciously, that the part of him that is lost is the mother. This can happen easily because in the symbiotic phase there is no differentiation yet between self and mother. As he starts to differentiate, and the mother becomes more of a separate person, he can only think that what he lost is his mother.

There is another subtle point in the symbiotic phase. The baby feels something has left him, and he sees the "good mother" as what has left him. In the symbiotic phase, he cannot have the conception that he lost something, because "he" as a separate person does not exist yet, not in his mind. So later on, when the individual contemplates the loss of merging essence, he can only think of it as loss of the "good mother." This is because he is now a separate individual and cannot function or operate as a dual unity, at least not consciously. In his deepest unconscious, the loss of merging essence is equated with the loss of the dual unity. (He cannot be conscious of this or he will lose his sense of being a separate individual.)

When merging love is lost, there is left in its place a vacuum, an emptiness, a hole in the being. Merging love of essence is a fullness—something is there. It is a delicate, soft fullness, a substantial presence. So its loss leaves an experience of an absence, a lack, that is acutely and painfully felt by the child. When an adult feels this emptiness or hole, it is usually experienced as an incompleteness, a lack, a deep deficiency.

This deficient emptiness is too painful for the child to endure. It is felt both emotionally and physically as painful. It is also experienced as a threat to the newly forming structure of the ego. This structure is still too weak and fragile to tolerate such loss, which happens right at the beginning stages of ego formation. The ego still needs the experience of gratifying symbiotic union for its wavering and fragile cohesion. To let itself feel fully the experience of loss of the merging essence, which is to the child's mind the complete loss of the "good mother," will be too shattering. The child still experiences the need for the "good mother" for his very survival, both physical and psychological, so really feeling the loss will bring in a great anxiety: the fear of total annihilation and dissolution.

Thus, the child learns not to feel the loss and the consequent emptiness. He learns to fill the emptiness, to cover it up, to bury it. He not only relegates it to the unconscious, he actually fills it with all kinds of emotions, beliefs, dreams, and fantasies.

There are two main ways a child can fill this hole, the absence of the merging essence. He either denies its existence completely and fantasizes the presence of the absent quality (here seen as the presence of the gratifying symbiotic union with mother), or he adopts attitudes, traits, mannerisms, dreams, and fantasies that are designed to regain the lost part. These are really attempts to regain the gratifying symbiotic unity with the mother. In the first case, he manufactures a false quality; in the second, he tries to get the merging by developing certain parts of his personality. Usually a child combines both strategies in differing proportions.

These attempts are designed to fill the hole, the lack resulting from the loss of the merging essence. The filler is nothing but parts of the personality. It is what the ego psychologists call self-representations. Edith Jacobson, one of the leading theoreticians in ego psychology, defines self-representation this way:

> From the ever-increasing memory traces of pleasurable and unpleasurable instinctual, emotional, ideational, and functional experiences, and of perception with which they become associated, images of the love objects as well as those of the bodily and psychic self emerge. Vague and variable at first, they gradually expand and develop into consistent and more or less realistic endopsychic representations of the object world and of the self.[4]

---

[4] Edith Jacobson, *The Self and the Object World* (New York: International Universities Press, 1980), 19.

We are not saying that all self-representations that make up the ego identity are attempts to fill this hole; some of the self-representations do not perform this function. But we are saying that what fills the hole becomes part of the self-representations. In fact, we assert that they form the most vital self-representations. Ego psychologists and object relations theorists do not say anything about holes or filling holes. They are not aware of the essence or of its loss. They do understand that the ego and its identity (self) are formed by the organization of self-representations.

"Shafer (1976), in his concern for a more precise use of the terms *self* and *identity*, writes: 'Self and identity serve as the super-ordinate terms for the self-representations that the child sorts out (separates, individuates) from its initially undifferentiated subjective experience of the mother-infant matrix.'"[5]

Here we are accepting completely this understanding of the development of the personality. We do not contradict any part of the object relations theory of the development of the personality. We are only adding the understanding that the main islands of self-representations, besides forming the sense of identity, function to fill the holes of essential losses. We have discussed so far the loss of merging love only. The loss of other aspects of essence leaves other holes and deficiencies.

Almost every human being fills the hole of merging love with certain sectors of the personality. Everybody loses the merging love aspect of essence through loss or frustration of the symbiotic union with the mothering person. Everybody is left with a hole. Everybody fills the hole by developing parts of the personality, either by false merging or attempts at getting their merged state. Variations will all be on the same theme.

We can see that the merging love issue is one of the main unconscious determinants motivating adults toward intimate love relationships and is also the reason behind many of the difficulties in relationships. It is well known in depth psychology that people see their mothers in their love partners. This happens, of course, because individuals deeply feel and believe that their incompleteness will be eliminated and their longing will be satisfied by regaining the

[5] Althea Horner, *Object Relations and the Developing Ego in Therapy* (New York: Jason Aronson, 1979), 11.

gratifying merged relationship with the mother, now displaced to a person of the opposite sex. This is probably the origin of the idea that a partner of the opposite sex is our "second half," or our complement.

What the person really wants and misses is part of his essence, the merging love, and is not the love partner or the relation with him or her. The individual believes that what is missing is the other half, or the intimate relationship, because that is what the child was able to see at the time of the original loss. The adult, like the child, does not know consciously that what is missing is part of oneself. So the search for fulfillment is directed outward, although the only thing that will actually work is the retrieval of the lost aspect of essence, the merging love. Therefore, intimate couple relationships will not be completely satisfying if the person is not able to experience this aspect of essence. The partner or the relationship cannot be but a poor substitute for the merging essence. And the partner will usually be blamed for the frustration, although the frustration doesn't have much to do with the partner. We are not condemning intimate love relationships or the desire for them; we are attempting to provide an understanding of one of their dynamics, a dynamic that usually causes great confusion and conflict about such relationships if not understood and resolved.

We have shown how a segment of the personality is developed as an aspect if essence is lost. It is possible to follow the vicissitudes of each essential aspect and see exactly the specific childhood situations that universally cause its loss. We will see that as each aspect of essence is lost, a certain hole or deficient emptiness is created. This is then filled by the development of a certain sector of the personality, a part of the personality determined by the particular aspect of essence lost, and by the specific childhood situation or situations that led to its loss.

In time, there will be no essence in the person's conscious experience. Instead of essence or being, there will be many holes: all kinds of deep deficiencies and lacks. However, the person will not usually be consciously aware of his perforated state. Instead, he is usually aware of the filling that covers up the awareness of these deficiencies, what he takes to be his personality. That is why this personality is considered a false personality by people aware of essence. The individual, however, honestly believes that what he is aware of is himself, not knowing that it is only a filling, layers of veils over the original experiences of loss. What is usually left of the experience of essence and its loss is a vague feeling of incompleteness, a gnawing sense of lack, that increases and deepens with age. However, this is true only for what is called the normal person, the adjusted personality, the standard of psychological balance in the culture.

But for many others, whose attempts at developing a personality were not as successful, where difficulties in childhood were too painful to make this personality work, the sense of deficiency and incompleteness is much more acute, much more painful, and much more incapacitating.

This state of taking the personality as the true identity and master of our life is what the Sufis call the state of sleep. The Sufi master Sanai of Afghanistan puts it this way: "Humanity is asleep, concerned only with what is useless, living in a wrong world."[6]

The essence is gone, and the personality claims its position. The shell claims to be the essence. The lie claims to be the truth. No wonder man is said to be living upside down. This situation is illustrated in graphic detail by a Sufi story that tells how the servants of a large house take it over when the master leaves for a long period. In time they forget that they are the servants; they forget their true positions and function. Eventually, they even believe they own the house.[7]

It is not possible for the average person who is identified with his personality to understand or appreciate the significance and the far-reaching consequences of this subversion. The average person actually, albeit mistakenly, believes that his personality is he himself. He has no context for comparing the experience of his personality with what he lost. He can only compare the experiences of his personality. The beauty and the wonder of essence is completely lost to him.

Repressing the various holes and the painful emotions around the losses necessitate that essence in its various aspects be repressed

---

[6] Idries Shah, *The Sufis*. Copyright © 1946 by Idries Shah. Reprinted by permission of Doubleday & Company, Inc. Excerpt, p. vii.

[7] Idries Shah, *The Sufis*, vii.

and cut off completely and efficiently. For if essence emerges into consciousness, it will ultimately bring to consciousness the deficiencies and the painful memories around it.

The human organism has in it many capacities for perception. The physical senses are the capacities available to ordinary humanity. However, there are many other organs or capacities for perception that are subtle and in a sense invisible. There are capacities for inner seeing, hearing, smelling, tasting, touching, and so on that have to do with the perception of the inner realm, that of the essence. There are capacities for intuition, direct cognition, synthesis, discrimination, and so on. All of these capacities are fueled by the substance of essence. Essence is what animates them. It is their life and light. This is what is hinted at in the Quranic light verse: "Allah is the light of heaven and earth. His light is like a lamp within a colored niche. The lamp is within a crystal, which is like a pearly heavenly body. It is lit from a blessed olive tree, not of the East or the West, whose oil itself nearly shines, without it being touched by any fire. Light upon light" (author's translation).

The organs of perception are, in fact, parts of essence; they are its organs and capacities. So when essence is cut off, the fuel of these capacities is gone, their light is dimmed, and most often goes out. The person loses not only his essence, but also his various subtle capacities and organs of perception and inner action.

These organs or capacities are connected to various energetic centers in the body that animate both the body and the mind. There are many and various centers as we discussed in Chapter Two, operating at different depths of the organism. There is the level of the chakras, which are centers connected to the various plexi of the nervous system. There is the deeper level of the lataif, which has some connection to the glandular system. There is the level that Gurdjieff used, the three centers in the belly, heart, and head. And there are other deeper levels of centers, which are invisible except to essence. To repress the essence completely and efficiently, these energetic and subtle centers have to be shut off, or at most allowed to operate at a minimum of activity and most of the time in distorted and unbalanced ways.

This leads to an overall desensitization and deadening of the body and its senses and to the narrowing and rigidifying of the mind and its activities. The person who knows only personality is not aware of how insensitive and callous he is. This is because he is not aware of how sensitive and refined he could be. He is not aware of how subtle, delicate, and clear his perceptions and actions could be. From the perspective of essence he is a brute, without sensitivity.

The loss of essence, the repression of the subtle organs and capacities, the shutting off and distortion of the subtle and energetic centers, and the overall resulting insensitivity, all lead to a general but devastating loss of perspective. The individual no more knows the point of life, of being, of existence. He no longer knows why he is living, what he is supposed to do, where he is going, let alone who he is. He is in fact completely lost.

He can only look at his personality, at the environment that created it, and live according to the standards of his particular society, trying all the time to uphold and strengthen his ego identity. He believes he is not lost because he is always attempting to live up to certain standards of success or performance, trying to actualize the dreams of his personality—yet all the time he is missing the point of it all.

It is no more the life of being; it is only the life of the personality, and in its very nature it is false and full of suffering. There is tension, contraction, restriction. There is no freedom to be and to enjoy. The true orientation toward the life of essence, the orientation that will bring about the life of the harmonious human being, is absent or distorted.

This loss of perspective and orientation leads to the loss of reality. The individual sees only illusions, follows only illusions, for he takes these illusions to be the reality. We are not talking here only about the neurotic or the pathological individual. Such a person, it is true, does not see the reality of the average and adjusted citizen of society. But this means he does not see the reality of the personality; his personality is incomplete, distorted, or too rigid.

Here we are mostly talking about the normal, adjusted person, one with a more or less complete and well functioning personality. This individual sees the reality of the personality only, and we have seen the truth of this reality, the truth about the personality: that it is not the being but is an impostor, pretending to be the truth.

The most important and tragic aspect of this loss of reality is the loss of what it is to be a complete human being, an individual who has not lost his human element, his essence. In a very real sense, an individual who is not connected to his essence is not a human being because the human element is one's essence. He is still a potential, a human in the seed stage. That is why some of the sages of the past have said that only the wise are human, "the wise" being those who are capable of knowing and being essence. El-Ghazali, the eleventh-century Sufi, puts it this way: "Wisdom is so important that it might be said that mankind is composed solely of the Wise."[8]

The condition of most humanity is even more tragic than this. It is not only that the person has lost his humanity; the individual has lost his existence, in the most real sense of the word. An individual who is not being, who is not being essence, is not really existing. He is not in touch with existence because existence, as we have seen, is the deepest aspect and characteristic of essence.

The experience of such an individual, whether normal or pathological, is the experience of the personality. As we have seen, the deepest nature of the personality is a deficiency, a hole, an absence, a nonexistence. So we can add to El-Ghazali's statement: Not only is it true that humanity consists solely of the wise, but also, in the most fundamental sense, only the wise exist.

---

[8] Idries Shah, *Thinkers of the East* (London: Johnathan Cape, 1971), 178.

CHAPTER FOUR

THE RETRIEVAL
OF ESSENCE

T MIGHT SEEM TO MANY that essence is fragile and that it is suppressed and easily lost. Essence is seen to be lost for almost everybody, and this fact might lead us to assume that it doesn't take much to suppress it. This, however, is just the appearance. To see the reality of the situation, a more penetrating and comprehensive look is necessary. A deeper investigation will show us that essence actually is not easily suppressed or lost. We will see instead that it takes a long time, with very powerful influences opposing it, for essence finally to recede and be buried.

One way to see this is to observe how resilient children are in their emotional health, their aliveness, their joy, and their passionate involvement in their activities. We see them bouncing back after many disappointments, many failures, and many discouragements. They bounce back to their aliveness and joy over and over for years before the aliveness and joy are slowly suppressed and lost. The fact is that it takes a hostile and contrary environment, continually and mercilessly rejecting, ignoring, and hurting the being of the child, for years on end, before it succumbs to suppression. The power, resilience, and strength of essence are enormous. It is the force of life itself, the mainspring of vitality and vigor.

But in almost all human communities it is hopelessly out-numbered and outmaneuvered until it is overwhelmed. Almost all forces and influences in the environment are hostile to it, and if not hostile, they are at least not understanding. Almost all forces—social, educational, religious, and even parental—are contrary or even hostile to the child's essence, wittingly or unwittingly. The child's essence is always misunderstood, ignored, or rejected, and frequently insulted, trampled, and hurt. We are not referring to isolated traumatic experiences only. We mean almost all of the time, in all interactions with the environment and the people in it.

This is because the environment is ruled by the personality, normal and pathological. All institutions of society, except for isolated instances, are formed, run, and populated by the personality, the usurper of the place of essence. And the personality by its very nature, by its existence, is contrary to the essence and lacks the understanding of its nature. Not only that, its very life is threatened by essence. For essence exposes its emptiness, bares its hurts, and makes transparent its falsehood. We saw in the previous chapter that the personality develops in the process of the loss of essence to fill the resulting void and to hide the painful deficiencies. It takes the place of essence. Its very basis is the absence of essence. Hence, these bases of its existence will be threatened by the emergence of essence. The personality cannot understand essence. It is in no position to sympathize with it and in most cases is in outright opposition to it.

We see here the plight of the child—his loneliness and isolation and the hopelessness of his position. For the child is still the essence, and regardless of how much the parents love their child, they are bound to misunderstand and suppress his being, the essence. Adults are mostly personality, and no matter how much they try, they will misunderstand and hurt the child's essence. They see reality from the perspective of the personality, and this perspective is based on the absence, not the existence, let alone the importance or the value, of essence.

The negative influences on the child's development resulting from the parents' lack of love, warmth, and positive regard are pretty much understood and appreciated by now. Modern depth psychology has shown in great detail how emotional conflicts and distortions of character mainly stem from early childhood experience. This knowledge has contributed a great deal to both therapy and education.

However, all this knowledge still relates to the personality and not to essence. The new understanding is about how difficulties in the personality arise and how measures can be taken to ameliorate such difficulties. The focus is still on the pathology of the personality, on its genesis, and on prophylaxis. This approach says nothing yet about essence.

A parent who is loving, caring, and supportive of the child helps the personality to grow more balanced and healthy and is less opposed to the beingness of the child. But this is still a far cry from actually seeing the essence, understanding it, and encouraging it to grow according to its own truth. Regardless of how loving the parents are toward their children, if the personality is the center of their life, the same will happen to the children. They will end up with the personality as the center, essence being buried.

So the problem is not a lack of good intentions and good will. It is a lack of something much more fundamental than that; it is the lack of the right orientation, the right perspective, and the right understanding. We saw in Chapter Two that most people do not recognize their essence. They also fail to recognize it in others, including their children. They wouldn't be able to even if they wanted to. In fact, they must ignore it, or they will have to confront their personality, with its losses and lacks.

We are not saying here that the personality has to be inimical and opposed to essence. We are pointing to the fact that it is usually so and that it is so primarily because it believes itself to be the true self and center of the human being. This usurpation of the position of essence (the servants becoming the masters of the house) creates a perspective and orientation contrary to that of essence.

Let's take an example to show the distortion of perspective. The personality can think only of self-esteem as a result of something, usually a result of certain actions and successes. The self-esteem of the individual rises, say, as a consequence of success in professional or social life. For the individual operating on a subtler level of existence, self-esteem rises as a result of living and acting according to one's own principles and convictions. At still deeper levels, self-esteem accrues as a result of being true to one's deepest feelings and stirrings.

All this is fine, understandable. However, it is not yet the perspective of essence. From the perspective of essence, that self-esteem is not a result of anything. Self-esteem, when it is real, is the value of essence. And the value of essence is nothing but essence itself in one of its aspects. Value, according to this perspective, is not something we gain; value is our nature. Essence is value. And if we try to get value as a result of something, then this value is not genuine. It is just filling a certain hole, the hole that resulted from the loss of our true value, an important aspect of our essence. In fact, any attempt to get value by excelling in any endeavor, inner or outer, will just cut us off from the true value, the absolute value of essence, where we *are* value, without this value being attributed to anything.

This is not an indictment of attempting excellence. It is separating excellence from the need for value. The correct relation is that excellence results from value and not the other way around.

THE DIAMOND APPROACH

The tremendous and omnipresent forces and influences that suppress essence are the same ones that work against retrieving it. Thus it is extremely difficult for most people to extricate themselves enough to taste essence or to know life from its perspective. In childhood, the forces were all external. But for the adult, these external forces have extended inward and have taken over the mind and the body. The individual in the process of ego development actually has imbibed his personality from the environment, and now he is the personality. The enemy of the essence is no more only in the environment. The greatest adversary now is one's own personality.

Now the personality, both inside and outside, works on all levels to solidify its position as the master and the center. The life becomes its life. This happens in all of the gross ways visible to us and in more subtle ways than can be seen by most people. Hence, the work on retrieving essence is primarily wrestling with the personality until it relinquishes its hold and surrenders its position to the true master, the human essence.

This endeavor, called the Work by most teachings oriented toward essence, becomes for the people who understand it the most worthy undertaking for man because without it man remains a potential, and the true human life is not realized. Without the realization of essence, every other undertaking is bound to be pointless, a waste. It is like an apple tree that is not allowed to bear apples. In fact, it is worse—it is like a larva that never becomes a butterfly.

Work systems and schools have existed throughout history and around the world, each deploying certain methods according to their particular ways of understanding the human situation. All of these methods are ways of dealing with the personality or going around it, or a combination of the two. The more successful approaches were usually the ones that were objective in their methods; objective in the sense that the minds of the people attempting to learn were taken into account, not only the subjectivity and the personal preferences of the teacher. The teaching and its methods were intelligently formulated and transmitted by taking into consideration the specific community involved and by paying attention to the time and place of the undertaking. This usually has to be done so that the teaching can be absorbed and digested by the particular mentality dominant in such a community at the specific time of the undertaking. This is a matter of skillful means to transmit the teachings of essence and its liberation in the most efficient way.

Older approaches can still be used to a certain extent, especially if modified to fit modern times and present communities. However, they are not expected to be as effective as they once were in their original homes at the times they were formulated. For instance, the old teachings of the Jewish cabbalists and the esoteric Christians were cast in the form of heaven and hell, populated by hierarchies of angels and devils. These formulations might still be useful in gaining certain insights and attitudes but will hardly be effective tools for a twentieth-century person to understand his life, let alone to use effectively for liberation. This understanding becomes even clearer when we consider, say, an American Midwesterner who is trying to understand and liberate himself using the Hindu images of Krishna and Shiva. Really to understand what these names stand for in the Indian mind he would have to understand the language and be steeped in and saturated by the Indian unconscious, which is full of the images of gods and goddesses. The images of Krishna and Shiva are accurately effective only in a mind whose unconscious developed in India, where these images formed part of the reality of childhood. Many people are still drawn to such ancient formulations, but that is mostly because of romantic and aesthetic considerations, not their effectiveness or efficiency.

Therefore, instead of discussing some of the various ancient methods of the Work, we will focus our attention on a specific approach, the Diamond Approach, formulated in the past decade, which takes into consideration the present situation. This situation is that humanity is steadily coming under the influence and the cultural dominance of Western civilization, with its science, technology, and rationality.

Although modern Western civilization is characterized mostly by its science and technology, the new understanding of the workings of the mind is equally significant. Depth psychology, pioneered by Sigmund Freud, has shed a great deal of light on a neglected aspect of the inner workings of the personality and on the dynamics of its development. It is definitely true, as some sources assert, that some of this knowledge was already known by some of the ancient schools of the Work. But these sources usually fail to acknowledge the new findings, findings that are so fundamental to the understanding of the mind and the personality that revisions in technique became imperative. It is true that the Buddhists had a good knowledge of how the mind operates phenomenologically, as attested by the texts of the Abhidharma. The Sufis understood conditioning, the functions of the emotions, and many other things. But it remained for Western depth psychology to discover and formulate in a very useful fashion the concepts of the unconscious, of repression, transference, psychodynamics, of the mental structure, and so on.

The nature of infantile sexuality and its importance for the development of the personality structure were never specifically understood before Freud. Now ego psychology, self psychology, and object relations theory, among others, have added to our knowledge a specific and profound understanding of how the personality and ego identity develop.

The ancients knew these things only vaguely and in the most general way. They had a basic understanding of the nature of personality that contemporary psychologists still lack; however, modern depth psychology has discovered and developed an understanding of the personality that the ancients did not imagine possible, regardless of how wise they were. Wisdom doesn't necessarily create understanding of the specifics, of how the human personality functions.

We are not here attempting to compare ancient psychology with modern depth psychology. The new psychological knowledge complements the old, basic wisdom. Many modern authors writing about Work methods tend to ignore or even disparage the latest monumental discoveries about the functioning of the mind and the development of the ego. But we believe this is because those authors have not been able to integrate this knowledge with their ancient wisdom. It is true that the new knowledge is incomplete and has many limitations, but this is true too of the ancient disciplines of the mind. Why not look objectively at what is available, and see the specific, even though limited, usefulness of each?

Let's look at a concrete example of how this can be done. In the chapter about the loss of essence, we discussed in some detail the vicissitudes of the essential aspect of merging love. This merging or melting essence, the clear, sweet, and golden essence, was obviously known by the teachers of the ancient schools, although understood by some and not by others. It is the force and the energy behind the desire for union with the universe, with God, with the primal intelligence, whatever. It was understood to be behind the longing for the disappearance into the Beloved. It is the love that melts the mind and the heart. Some probably understood its specific action of melting and dissolving ego boundaries and attempted to invoke it to facilitate surrender.

However, it wasn't possible to understand its significance for the development of the ego until the advent of ego psychology and especially of Margaret Mahler's monumental work on the development of the ego, formulated by her as the process of separation–individuation. She formulated the symbiotic stage as a phase of the process of development characterized by the absence of differentiation and boundaries for the ego. This formulation enables us to see the significance of merging love for the process of ego development, and for the structure of ego identity.

It is understood now that the symbiotic stage is of paramount importance for the development of the personality and the ego identity.

> Within the symbiotic orbit, the two partners or poles of the dyad may be regarded as polarizing the organizational and structuring processes. The structures that derive from this double frame of reference represent a framework to which all experiences have to be related before there are clear and whole representations in the ego of the self and

the object world (Jacobson, 1964). Spitz (1965) calls the mother the auxiliary ego of the infant. Similarly, we believe the mothering partner's holding behavior, her 'primary maternal preoccupation' in Winnicott's sense (1958), is the symbiotic organizer—the midwife of individuation, of psychological birth.[1]

So ego identity is seen to originate in this time of undifferentiated dual unity. In fact, the deepest aspects of the personality are seen to go back to this undifferentiated state of the ego. The personality began to be absorbed particularly at that time, between two and ten months of age. In fact, undifferentiation, or merging, is necessary for this absorption of the qualities of the personality. Personality, then, begins with the child's identification with the qualities that the child experiences through merging with the environment. During the merged condition of the symbiotic stage, the child has no conception of what is his and what belongs to the environment represented by the mother. There is still no concept of self and other. This is the meaning of dual unity. So a feeling that might originate in the mother could end up as the child's. The child experiences the feeling because of the merged condition. If in time he identifies with it, it becomes his. In fact it becomes part of his developing personality.

The ego psychologists understand symbiosis but are not aware that it is made possible by the presence of the essential aspect of merging love. They see the external manifestations of the presence of this essential aspect. They are not aware of its actual presence or even of its possibility. In other words, they see the lack of differentiation and boundaries, but they take this as all that is happening. They are, quite naturally, not aware that this lack of differentiation goes along with an actual presence in the child that has the characteristic of melting boundaries. Ancient wisdom, on the other hand, is aware of this aspect of essence and understands its effect of melting away boundaries but is not aware of the symbiotic stage as a phase of ego development. However, now that we have both kinds of understanding, we can see the relation of this particular aspect of essence to the development of the ego; we can see how it affects this development, when and why, as we have seen in the last chapter.

---

[1] Margaret S. Mahler et al., *The Psychological Birth of the Human Infant* (New York: Basic Books, 1975), 47.

So now we not only have the understanding of how the personality develops, but by integrating the knowledge of essence, we can understand this development in relation to the various aspects of essence. This understanding is specific enough to trace the vicissitudes of essential qualities or aspects throughout the stages of ego development.

This understanding of how the personality develops as essence is lost is the outcome of integrating the ancient wisdom with modern depth psychology. Of course, this is not the whole story of the development of personality. Personality development also can be understood from the point of its necessity for physical survival and of the organism's need to deal with its external environment. We are here highlighting only the dynamics of its genesis and development in relation to the being, the essence.

This way of seeing the matter produces a methodology for the return to essence that is understandable by and congruent with modern human mentality. It takes into consideration how man in this era understands things and what kinds of concepts govern his mind. But before we go into the specific details of this method we call the Diamond Approach, let's see how some of the ancients worked to realize the particular essential aspect of merging love. This will help us later on for purposes of contrast.

Because this aspect of essence has the effect on the nervous system of producing feelings of sweetness and love and the attitude of humility, and because at the same time it affects the ego by melting its structural boundaries, some of the ancient approaches were emotional and devotional in nature. Prayer, supplication, devotional singing and dance, all directed toward a beloved deity or reality, served to melt the heart and put the mind in a set receptive to this essential aspect. In other words, these methods are designed to put the mind and heart (the nervous system) in the same condition that is produced by the actual presence of this essential aspect. This allows the possibility of its manifestation. In such practices, the personality is, in a sense, transcended or put aside, and the aspirant attempts to cultivate attitudes more receptive to the essential reality, attitudes that might actually be contrary to the structure of the personality.

Other methods, like the yogic ones, see that the personality is the barrier to essence. They see, with the subtle organs of perception, where the particular essential aspect operates in the subtle physiology, and they see the personality barrier as certain dark spots that clog the relevant subtle channels and their corresponding parts of the nervous system. Then certain exercises—breathing techniques, postures, visualizations, and chants—are devised either to penetrate through the dark spots and blow them up or to reroute the energy around them and therefore not have to deal with them directly. Then the energy is concentrated at the specific locations where the essential aspect will most likely and most strongly operate. We see this in the following quotation from a Taoist text concerning the cultivation of this aspect, which the text calls the golden elixir, or golden nectar:

> Question: What is the macrocosmic alchemical agent and how can one transmute it into golden nectar and return the latter to the cauldron (in the abdomen)?
>
> Answer: The Macrocosmic alchemical agent is the union of both outer and inner microcosmic agents which emits the light of reality. The nectar (or sweet dew, kan lu) is produced long after the intermingling of the four symbols (prenatal heaven and earth and postnatal heart and abdomen) and the union of the sun with the moon (the positive yang and negative yin). He who knows how to gather it will obtain the golden nectar but he who does not gets only the white one (pure saliva). If it is young the light is blurred and unstable in the chung kung cavity (solar plexus). This (circle of) light manifests in the condition of utter stillness but if it grows from a small to a larger one and then vanishes, or if it shrinks from a large to a small one, splits into three, or looks like a crescent, all this shows that the generative force and vitality are not full. But if the light suddenly goes up and down so quickly that the eyes cannot follow it, it is imperative to gather vitality immediately and return the circle of light to the body. Then after his heart and intellect have settled the practiser should roll his eyes from A to D, G, J, and back to A, as follows:

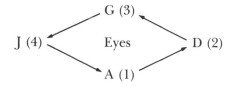

After rolling his eyes, he should close them and as his mouth is now full of golden nectar, he should make pointed concentration on the vitality which he has just circulated (as above), driving it down (the jen mo or channel of function), followed by the golden nectar, into the cavity of vitality (below the navel). This is returning vitality to the cauldron to seal it.[2]

We see here a very careful and calculated technique for routing a specific energy and concentrating it through some of the channels of the subtle physiology, so that a certain alchemical process will commence and produce the golden elixir. This careful and elaborate setup is necessary in such a method to force the energy to flow in a specific channel, because if it does not, it will be blocked in the places in the body where the personality barriers are strong. So the whole method is a way of going around the barriers to get to the goal. We see here the extreme difficulty of performing and staying with such a task, and we see why many years of preparation are generally required. Usually, the chances of success are very meager in this sort of method and in the devotional methods mentioned above. This is because the personality is everywhere in the body and mind, and its barriers are omnipresent. They are so subtle that most practitioners get bogged down without quite knowing what has stopped their progress.

There are, of course, many other old methods for realizing this essential aspect, but we are considering here just a few, to illuminate more effectively the modern approach we are about to discuss.

According to the Diamond Approach, the barriers of the personality to the merging love aspect (and to all others), these dark spots and knots that clog the flow of energies, are nothing but certain specific mental and emotional contents relating to the loss of the essential aspect and the subsequent attempts at compensation. In other words, the dark spots are areas of darkness in our personality: certain emotions, memories, and ideas that are cut off from consciousness and repressed. What the yogis see is the repressed unconscious content, but they understand it only energetically and not psychologically. In our approach, we use psychodynamic understanding to see through these dark spots and dissolve them. The

---

[2] Charles Luk, *Taoist Yoga* (York Beach, ME: Samuel Weiser, 1970), 73.

spots are dark because they are repressed material; the light of awareness and understanding does not reach them. So we open each knot, and shed the light of awareness on its content. This will bring out to consciousness the relevant repressed memories and affects. The discharge, the actual experiencing and understanding of this content, usually dissolves the dark spots. In this way we go on dissolving one barrier after another until the whole channel is clean. There is no need here for the extreme caution that the yogis require because we can shed light on and open any dark spot that confronts us. We don't need to go around or avoid anything. This method is a direct confrontation with the personality, understanding any part of it that comes within the field of our awareness.

Of course we don't need to see the actual dark spots in the nervous system, although it is possible. They manifest to us psychologically, usually as resistances, emotional defenses, and their corresponding repressed material. By applying our awareness and understanding, barrier after barrier will surface and be dismantled, until finally the merging love aspect of essence will be released.

Some will object that there is nothing new in this method. That it is just a certain way of seeing methods used already by many. For instance, that is how psychoanalysis and psychotherapy work and how character analysis and Reichian therapy work on the muscular armor.

It is true; there is nothing new yet except a different way of seeing things, in terms of the subtle physiology. However, we still haven't used our understanding of the development of the personality in relation to essential aspects. Here the specificity, the exactness, and the power of the method will become obvious.

We have seen how the personality develops by following the vicissitudes of essential aspects. The current psychoanalytic method is to go backward, to retrace our steps, to regress. This regression, this retracing of our steps, is the same as going along the subtle channels and dissolving the dark spots, with one difference. In the Diamond Approach, there is now a knowledge of which essential aspect is connected with each of these spots. The actual content of the dark areas is now known specifically for each aspect. Let's continue the example of the merging essence.

On the surface we find the person having difficulties with merging. He cannot experience merging essence, although he wants it and longs for it. This longing could be conscious, in which case the person is usually going after the experience of merging in all kinds of ways, but never really zeroing in on exactly what he wants. He is looking for closeness, intimacy, warmth, love, acceptance. He has difficulties in asserting himself, in taking his own space in any situation of separateness and distance. He is always looking for the magical love relationship that will finally melt away all of his worries and difficulties, in which he can rest and be happy and be himself. But he consistently has conflicts around these relationships, such as always feeling dissatisfied, discontented, and incomplete.

On the other hand, longing might be unconscious, with the person defending against closeness, tenderness, melting, and love. He is afraid of dependency and is proud of his strength and independence. He seeks separateness and defends it with his life.

In the psychodynamic approach, the second kind of person needs first to see through his defenses, which is his first dark spot. This means he has to see through his pride, his false independence, and his defensive separateness. In this process, he will undoubtedly confront great and deep fears, for instance, the fear of being weak, dependent, and helpless.

In both cases, the person will have to observe and understand all of the ways he tries to achieve the merged experience. He will have to understand his behavior in intimate or sexual relationships. He will have to understand his feelings of liking compulsively close and intimate communities, his idealizations of brotherly feelings, or his compulsive idealization of unification and bringing people or things together. All these will be seen as ways of acting out the feelings of deficiency, the emptiness resulting from the essential loss.

When these ways of acting out are seen as expressions of the deficiency and not of fullness, as the person would like to believe, he will have the chance to be free from indulging in this wasteful and defensive acting out. He will experience the deficiency itself, the emptiness, the hole. This is the content of one of the main dark spots. The individual will start feeling impoverished, dependent, needy, cold, and empty.

This emptiness will actually be experienced as a cavity, an absence of fullness, if the person succeeds in not defending against it. The person will experience a hole, a cavity in the energy system of the organism, usually centered in the lower part of the chest. This particular hole, specific to the merging essence, is connected with a subtle center located in this area at the place where the diaphragm meets the sternum.

At this point the person might go on to experience himself as an empty space, devoid of any fullness or quality. If he deals with the associations he has to this emptiness—such as those of dependency and need—and the fears produced by them—probably the fears of disintegration, disappearing, and so on—then he will remember the old hurt that cut off the essence. This is another big dark spot. The person will unearth the painful situation or situations that ultimately led to the loss of this particular aspect of essence. Besides the memories and affects, the individual will experience the emotional hurt as a wound. It will feel physically like a wound in the chest, but it is a wound in the energy system that corresponds to the emotional hurt and the loss of the essence. When one allows oneself quietly to experience the hurtful wound and the memories connected with it, the golden elixir will flow out of it, healing it, and filling the emptiness with the beautiful sweet fullness that will melt the heart, erase the mind, and bring about the contentment that the individual has been thirsting for.

The flow of the merging essence will happen when the individual feels and realizes exactly what he actually wanted and couldn't have as a child of a year or so. As we know, the merging essence is connected in the symbiotic phase with the dual unity, with the gratifying merging with the mother. This means that here, in the depth of the hurt, in the middle of the bleeding wound, the individual will realize: "I want my mommy, I love my mommy." When this is deeply felt, now that all of the barriers are gone, the merging essence will emerge, because for the baby the merging essence is Mommy.

As we see, the individual will have to retrace his steps, regress his personality to the time of the symbiotic state, and there he will find this sweet part of himself, just the way he had it then. Now it is unearthed, dug out from its burial place, and released.

We see from this example why it is so difficult to gain access to essence using the old methods. There is a great deal of repression and defense in the way of the experience of essence. And it is not easy to ignore or go around all of this repression, all of these barriers that are omnipresent in the organism. We also see why most people won't even commit themselves to this journey, a journey that involves confronting terrible fears. How can a person who is deeply afraid that he will disintegrate sit and meditate quietly? The fear of disintegration is one of the obstacles that must be surmounted in the process of opening the centers to the flow of essence. This fear is compounded because it is unconscious and therefore irrational.

The merging essence is repressed at the symbiotic stage of the process of ego development. At this stage, the ego has not developed as a separate entity on its own. Regressing to this stage means the ego must regress to the form it had before it developed into a cohesive entity. Of course, this will arouse the ego's fear of loss of cohesion, loss of integration, and loss of its object status. In fact, the person must experience and tolerate the disintegration, which, if understood, will turn out to be nothing but experiencing himself as empty space. Space is actually the nature of the mind without structure. So how can a person who has this fear but does not know that he has it be able to sit and meditate or kneel in prayer! How can he quietly do some yogic exercises when this terrible unfathomable fear is approaching consciousness without the person having the slightest inkling of what it is all about!

Under most circumstances the individual does not get close to this fear, and hence does not get close to the merging essence. On approaching it, psychological defenses will surface, which the person will experience as all kinds of barriers. These barriers can be overcome only in unusual circumstances, under a very strict discipline, with a very good guide.

However, in using a psychodynamic approach the defenses will be analyzed and understood. The fears will be seen in their true perspective, which will allow the individual to confront and experience them in a much easier way.

This method might appear to be a kind of psychotherapy, but it is really not so. In fact, it is a different kind of thing, although it does use psychological understanding and techniques.

Psychotherapy does not acknowledge the existence of essence or the loss of essence; therefore it is not oriented toward retrieving it. Psychotherapy is oriented toward making the personality healthier and stronger, making it function better. In dealing with merging essence, psychotherapy does not usually go beyond the first step. The empty hole is almost never approached. Rather, the person learns to find better and more effective ways to fill the hole, which are seen as better relationships with people or a more satisfying intimate relationship with a person of the opposite sex.

Some therapies involve the exploration of the individual's past and his relationship to his mother. Even his symbiotic relationship with his mother might be explored. But since the symbiotic stage is not seen to be connected to the merging essence, the exploration becomes confined to the relationship itself, to its gratifications and its frustrations. Then, by seeing and understanding this relationship and experiencing some of the affects associated with it, the conflicts within the personality will be ameliorated, and the person will be better able to function in relation to others. The whole approach of therapy works toward lifting some of the repression against the emotions, or modifying the structure of the personality slightly so it can function better.

In fact, the accepted attitude in psychoanalysis and the various other psychotherapies is that dealing with issues relating directly to the symbiotic stage is relevant only for the severe pathologies, such as the borderline and psychotic syndromes. It is believed that normal or neurotic people don't usually need to deal deeply with issues of the symbiotic stage. These people do not experience important conflicts around this stage because the personality structure has developed solidly from it. For psychotherapy, there is no need then to go to such depths for normal people because they function well in terms of their ego structure.

But our concern here is not therapy. Our aim is much more fundamental; it is the return to being. From our perspective, anybody who has lost the merging essence and wants to regain it must go back to the symbiotic stage and deal with its issues. And this is true for normal people, those who are neurotic, and everybody else, not just for the severe psychopathologies. In fact, we will see that if a person involves himself with the journey of return using the psychodynamic approach, the issues explored will be mostly what are usually considered in psychoanalytic circles as borderline, narcissistic, and psychotic issues. This means that all people, not just the ones afflicted with pathology, are narcissistic, borderline, and psychotic. However, these tendencies, termed *the psychotic core*, are buried very deeply in the unconscious, and the normal person never really deals squarely with these underpinnings of his character. Neither, of course, does he come to live the life of essence, unless he sincerely embarks on doing the work.

Narcissistic pathology, borderline syndrome, and the psychoses are nothing but failures and deficiencies of the structure of the personality itself, as is becoming understood now in depth psychology. The work on essential development involves actually confronting and softening this same structure. It does not only modify it but in some sense actually dismantles the ego identity and reinstitutes the lost identity, the true, high self of the essence. This is bound to bring to consciousness all the conflicts, fears, distortions and deficiencies in the structure.

We are not here lauding weak or deficient structures of the personality; borderline tendencies and psychosis are not essence. They are just rips in the structure of the personality itself. Actually, the personality must be somewhat stable but flexible for the work of essential development to be possible. Otherwise, the conflicts and fears will be too quickly disintegrating, and the person will not be able to tolerate the process.

The process of essential retrieval and development does not require complete and permanent dissolution of the personality. Rather, it needs a personality strong enough and flexible enough to allow temporary dissolution and regrouping, so that the relation between the personality and the essence will change. What really needs to happen is that the personality assume the role and position of the servant to essence, not its master. The personality will be in the service of essence, doing its true and natural function.

In some circumstances in deep psychotherapy, especially in depth psychoanalysis or Reichian vegetotherapy, the patient might even contact the deficiency itself, which we described above as the emptiness, or hole. The deficiency is, however, not allowed to expand to the point of the patient feeling himself as empty space. This would bring about terrible fears of disintegration, which the therapist himself cannot tolerate. The possibility of a temporary complete dissolution of the personality is not envisioned, and so neither the patient nor the therapist can actually allow the experience. The therapist usually is not aware of the possibility of experiencing oneself as empty space, as the void. He will have to deal with his own fears and conflicts to be able to allow his patient to go through the experience. So the emptiness might be allowed emotionally but never on the fundamental phenomenological dimension.

Even if the patient goes beyond the emptiness to the dimension of essence, the therapist will not be able to acknowledge or understand the patient's experience. We believe that essence experiences do occur once in a while in therapy sessions. But because the therapist is not trained to recognize the essence, what he will see and acknowledge will be the effect of the essence on the nervous system: the feelings of love and contentment. Because the essence is not recognized, the effect of the therapist on the patient will be similar to that of the loving parent on the child. There will be acceptance, understanding, and warmth, but only toward the personality. The essence will still be ignored and not understood. This will automatically reinstate the repressive forces.

The fact is that for the therapist actually to see, understand, and acknowledge essence, he himself should have experienced it in his own body; otherwise, he will be threatened by it. Most likely he will take his patient's perceptions of merging essence as a hallucination. How else can he take it? He does not know that there is such a thing as essence, let alone a substance that is not physical.

The barriers against the experience of essence in the therapeutic situation are many. In the case of the merging essence we can see one specific but important barrier. The merging essence melts away ego boundaries and allows a condition of merging to take place. So if the merging essence arises in the patient, he will automatically and unconsciously merge with the energy system of the therapist. Since the therapist has his own barriers and fears regarding this essential aspect, the patient will experience them. He also will experience them as his own because of the merging condition, and this will block his experience again. In this circumstance, the barriers of the therapist serve to repress the essence of the patient, without either of them knowing it.

On the other hand, if a person is working with a competent teacher of the Work, the teacher is not only not blocked against this aspect of essence but when the student's essence emerges, the same quality of the teacher's essence will come forth strongly and spontaneously and will, both consciously and unconsciously, encourage and support the student's experience. Instead of blocking the emerging essence of the student, he will support it, even without uttering a word. He is really a midwife in such a situation, in the deepest sense here, in a sense that is unequaled anywhere else.

This is in no way a diminution or a disparaging of the therapist and his function. His job is therapy and not the Work. But the person who is interested in regaining essence and who undergoes psychotherapy must understand this distinction clearly. Confusion arises these days because of the proliferation of growth systems, and the attitude of looking at therapy as "growth process." Therapy can function for growth, but we must remember that the Work is for the growth of the essence, not the personality.

There is a subtle gray area between the two orientations that is at present confusing many people. This confusion involves the experience of emotional discharge or energetic release. This discharge, or release—whether it is called expression, streaming, or whatever—produces a momentary sense of relief and freedom. Because of this sense of freedom, it is considered by some as work on freeing the essence. However, it is not necessarily, and most often it in fact is not, a freeing of the essence. Usually, it is a release from the restricting tensions of the personality. Such experiences typically involve some release of bodily tensions and a freer flow (sometimes temporary, sometimes more stable) of physical energies. This can be useful for the Work if it is seen in its correct perspective as a preparation, a prelude for the emerging of essence. Freedom is first a freedom *from*—from the personality. Later it is a freedom *for*—for the essence to be.

Thus, we see that psychotherapy, from the perspective of the Work, stops short of essential realization. In a very fundamental way, it is unable to fulfill man's deepest longing. It can, when successful, help the personality to function more efficiently and more harmoniously. But from the perspective of the Work, we ask: To what end? The most worthy undertaking is still not attempted. The human essence still remains a potential, unactualized. As Idries Shah puts it, "It is impossible, from this point of view, to attempt to restore a mere equilibrium without a dynamic forward movement. The psychologist tries to make a warped wheel turn smoothly. The dervish is trying to make the wheel turn in order that it may propel a carriage."[3]

It is not only that psychotherapeutic endeavors don't lead to essence; they are, contrary to all assertions, rarely ever effective in completely resolving any of the deep conflicts of the patient. The deepest and most fundamental human conflicts can be resolved completely only when the corresponding essential aspects are regained and established. Take our example of the merging essence. The conflicts around it, about merging and separation, intimacy and

---

[3] Idries Shah, *The Sufis*. Copyright 1946 by Idries Shah. Reprinted by permission of Doubleday & Company, Inc. Excerpt, p. 276.

autonomy, and so on cannot be resolved; in fact, they cannot be understood unless the merging essence itself is realized. The merging essence is the only true resolution of these conflicts. Its loss is what brought about the deficiency and the corresponding emotional patterns. Only regaining it will eliminate the deficiency and the corresponding personality patterns. Also, how can there be understanding of these conflicts if some of the necessary data, the knowledge of the merging essence, are not available?

Psychotherapy's goal is to resolve the conflicts only on the psychological level. It attempts this by working on understanding the conflicts and their origins in childhood. It believes that through this understanding and the discharge of repressed emotions, the conflicts will be resolved. But how can that be, when the most fundamental point in the conflict is the loss of the essence? The individual knows, although unconsciously, what he has lost. His personality is always subtly irritated by the hole in his chest. He will feel complete, he will be completely contented about this conflict, only if he regains what he has lost. There is no other way. Understanding or no understanding, completion and contentment will happen only when there is a hole no more, only when essence is there, experienced and acknowledged.

The deepest cause of all conflicts of the personality is the loss of essence. It is not childhood programming; childhood programming leads to the loss of essence. It is this loss that is the greatest deficiency. From this perspective, we see that depth psychology itself has a hole, a deficiency. This deficiency is the absence of essence in its understanding.

The essence here is not only one element of the personality's conflicts, it is the biggest piece of the puzzle. Without this biggest piece, without this missing element, the puzzle can never be solved and completed.

We have described the Diamond Approach only in terms of dealing with one aspect of essence, the merging love. This example illustrates only generally how the method works. We could have used any other aspect of essence, such as peace, awakeness, will, joy, strength, compassion, essential personality, or essential identity. Instead, we have chosen the example of merging love because most people can relate to the issues surrounding it. However, for the student involved in the Work, the method is applied and used to regain all the aspects of essence and then used to establish them permanently.

We have shown how this method is different from the psychotherapeutic approaches and how it is also different from the old traditional methods of the Work. This method integrates and synthesizes in one organic approach the two above disciplines. Combining the knowledge of the two fields in a unitary method, it achieves therapeutic results, but its aim is the bigger and more fundamental one of essential development.

The Diamond Approach, because it integrates the findings of depth psychology into the methodology of the Work, makes the latter more accessible to a wider range of interested students. It spans the range of human development because it adds the knowledge of the personality. The genuine traditional systems had to choose from the applicants only the healthiest and the most balanced, or sometimes the most desperate, for there was no sufficient understanding of the less fortunate or less determined and no methods available to help them.

Also, this method avoids the pitfalls of some of the traditional methods. Those traditional methods left room for experimentation by amateurs, and this posed a danger for themselves in case they were successful in realizing some of the subtle energies and capacities without the necessary knowledge, guidance, and preparation. Idries Shah, for instance, refers to this danger after discussing the Sufi system of development: "Attempts to cause the self to operate out of sequence, . . . produces the sort of confusion—and sometimes worse—which is reflected in some current literature of experimenters who choose their own sequence of events, and may cause developments which they cannot handle."[4]

In the Diamond Approach there is no room for experimentation. The method itself is not mechanical, is not an exercise. It requires sincerity and a willingness to confront one's personality and to deal with conflicts before essence or the lataif can be released. In other words, in this method, essence is released by using understanding. And this understanding concerns exactly the sectors of the personality that will usually arise and create trouble for the amateur using quasi-mechanical methods. So it has its own safeguards built in as part of its structure.

These barriers in the personality also will arise even if the person is not an amateur but is practicing one of the traditional methods in a Work school or under the guidance of a teacher. This

---

[4] Idries Shah, *A Perfumed Scorpion* (London: Octagon Press, 1978), 84.

arising unconscious material must be dealt with; otherwise, the emerging essence will be repressed and buried again.

The bringing forth of unconscious material happens, of course, in the Diamond Approach. For instance, new issues and side conflicts arise after the merging essence emerges. The method, as we have described it so far, has dealt with the main issue: the unconscious symbiotic wish for the mother. But there are many other associated issues that will surface from the unconscious now that the central knot in this complex is untied. This, of course, presents new material that can lead the student to broader and deeper understanding.

Psychodynamic understanding continues to be applied, to discover and resolve the surfacing issues. This process, which is analogous to what in psychoanalysis is called the process of working through, will eventually establish the relevant essential aspect. This is the process referred to by the Sufis as the changing of a state into a "station," that is, a permanently available condition. This process also will reach other threads in the structure of the personality and so will lead to other essential aspects, until they are all established. This is the process of the development of essence, which takes us to the next chapter.

CHAPTER FIVE

THE DEVELOPMENT OF ESSENCE

N THE LAST CHAPTER we discussed the way of return to essence, to our being. We have discussed in particular a certain psychodynamic method, the Diamond Approach. This approach is based on the understanding of how essence is lost, as we described it in Chapter Three. We have discussed so far the most crucial aspect of this method, the process of the recovery and retrieval of the buried essence. This approach implies theoretically and demonstrates in practice that essence can never be totally, literally lost. What happens is that it gets buried, covered over by layers of the personality—essence becomes repressed, relegated to the unconscious. That is precisely why a psychodynamic approach can be effective. Psychodynamic methods are based on the topology of the mind, as Freud formulated it. They assume that part of the mind is conscious and another part, where conscious awareness does not penetrate, is unconscious.

On this matter we differ from Freud only in that we see that the unconscious includes in it the essence itself. Freud looked at the mind and concluded that parts of its tripartite structure—the id, ego, and superego—are buried in the unconscious. But like most Western depth psychologists, his understanding of the mind constrained him from going beneath the level of the chakra system. He stayed within the realm of the personality and its instinctual sources, which do not operate deeper than the chakra system. However, his topological and structural point of view is very useful for us, as we have already seen and as we will further see as we discuss the continuing development of essence. Since essence becomes repressed (as do affects, ideas, and fantasies), the job of retrieving essence becomes simple and obvious: to make the unconscious conscious. This will, however, alter the structure of the personality itself and will change its position in the overall economy of the human organism. This is because, as we discussed in Chapter Three, the structure of the personality is based in large part on the experience of the loss of essence. So when essence is unrepresssed and freed, it will change the personality structure.

AWARENESS

This simple dictum, to make the unconscious conscious, is the most fundamental, basic, and necessary aspect of the Diamond Approach and of all other genuine methods of the Work. The individual begins with consciousness and ends with consciousness—consciousness is simply expanded further and further. We must point out here that by consciousness we mean awareness, because the word *consciousness* is sometimes used to denote other concepts. Some authors, in fact, use the word *consciousness* to refer to essence.

Therefore, as in all systems of inner development, to apply the Diamond Approach, the individual cultivates awareness. The main method is to erase unconsciousness through psychodynamic techniques. However, even to start this process, the person must learn how to pay attention, how to be aware of inner and outer happenings. Awareness is needed to collect observations that can then be used for the psychodynamic understanding. Without awareness, the person will not know what thoughts go through his mind, what emotions fill his heart, or what sensations there are in his body. So there will be no impression, no material for understanding, if there is not enough awareness.

The ordinary person has awareness, but it is very restricted, confined, and selective. In awareness training, the individual learns to expand his awareness, to let it not be confined by his habitual and compulsive patterns. As awareness is freed more and more, the powers of observation expand, and the material for understanding becomes more available.

Awareness is necessary not just for collecting observations for the process of understanding but really for all aspects of the work of inner development. It is also, of course, necessary for everyday practical living. Awareness is a characteristic of life itself, of all living matter.

The cultivation of awareness is necessary also for its own sake. Ultimately, awareness itself is an aspect of essence, necessary in its own right, as a part of our very being. Awareness is a basic characteristic of all aspects of essence. Essence is spontaneously self-aware. However, awareness can exist on its own. In other words, an individual can experience himself as awareness, as just pure, naked awareness.

Awareness occupies a very special place among essential aspects. In a sense, inner development as a whole—the work on both personality and essence—can be seen as the freeing and the expansion of awareness. The reason behind this is that the most basic function of the personality is the reduction of awareness. In fact, the deepest aspect of the personality is a restriction of awareness. The ego identity, which normally is called the self, exists on the deepest level as a contraction of awareness, a restriction of consciousness. To say it more accurately, the ego identity (the I) as a structure is on the deepest level a hole of awareness, or a deficiency of awareness, because of the loss of intrinsic and basic awakeness. This is the deepest and most defended hole in the personality.

This deepest hole in the personality, around which its identity is structured, is the avoidance (the loss) of the awareness of death. More accurately, the personality does not understand death, and it avoids the perception of its possibility and its existence. It is terrified of death because it means its own annihilation. We are not referring here to the death of the body, although the personality cannot conceive of any other kind of death because of its identification with the body. We mean the experience of nonexistence, which is the absence of experience. But this nonexistence is the deepest nature of the personality, its very center.

The personality's fear and avoidance of death creates a gap (a hole) in awareness around which the personality is structured. This gap is the kernel of the unconscious. Unconsciousness develops as the personality develops and is structured around this hole. Unconsciousness is ultimately unconsciousness of death, which is necessitated by the lack of understanding of what death is.

So we can say that inner development is the expansion of awareness. Complete awareness is just that. It excludes nothing, not even the direct awareness of nonexistence (death). The Work is the expansion of awareness until the personality becomes aware of its most hidden secret, death. When this is revealed, there will be no fear in the personality; fears start dropping away. And then the deepest contraction and tension in the personality, which is the avoidance of the awareness of death, is loosened. This leads to the loosening of identification with the personality, because the identification is based on this deepest contraction within the personality. This in turn helps the essence to attain its true position as master.

This deepest secret in the unconscious of the personality, like the rest of its deep and repressed sectors, is so inaccessible to the ordinary consciousness and so defended against that it is practically impossible to reach. Relying solely on the direct cultivation of awareness is in most instances not sufficient to penetrate these deepest recesses of the mind. This is one reason the systems that work only on cultivating awareness turn out not to be so efficient in inner development.

Here we find one of the greatest uses of essence. Essence can penetrate to these deep, dark corners of the personality. Essence can go all the way because it *is* the deep. And because essence is intrinsically characterized by awareness, it can take our consciousness to these deep and normally inaccessible places of the unconscious and expose them to observation and understanding. This will in turn expose more holes, so that new and deeper aspects of essence are retrieved.

We see here a reciprocal process, in which understanding the personality brings out the essence, and then the essence brings out deeper layers of the personality and so on. This process continues, and awareness expands, until all of the personality is understood, all the way to the experience of its own death and nonexistence. In addition, all aspects of essence will be recognized and developed in the process. This naturally sets the ground for the spontaneous arising of the perception of enlightenment.

We see here a glimpse of the great assistance that essence provides for the work of freedom from the personality, the condition of enlightenment. We are stressing this point because much of Work literature makes it sound as if the Work is designed to accomplish freedom from personality and then the development of essence. Although this is possible, it is very unlikely and happens extremely rarely because of the complexity, depth, and subtlety of the personality. In this method, the Diamond Approach, there is no need to wait for the experience of ego death before one understands essence. A person can traverse the path by going through small "deaths," which will bring out the aspects of essence, which will in turn lead to the final experience of ego death.

SENSITIVITY AND THE SUBTLE PERCEPTIONS

A major necessary part of awareness training is the sensitization of the body. The tendency toward insensitivity needed to support unconsciousness has to be reversed. Repression and the defenses of the ego are not just mental attitudes. They are, more than anything else, tensions and tension patterns in the body. These physical blocks and tensions are what keep emotions and ideas unconscious. This point was emphasized by Wilhelm Reich in his formulation of the concept of character armor and muscular armor. His main insight was that the defensive functions of the character are identical with muscular rigidities in the body: "In character-analytic practice, we discover the armor functioning in the form of a chronic, frozen, muscular-like bearing. First and foremost, the identity of these various functions stands out; they can be comprehended on the basis of one principle only, namely of the armoring of the periphery of the biopsychic system."[1]

Emotions and feelings are primarily sensations, and these are sensations of the body. If the body is insensitive, there will be no awareness of these sensations and hence no awareness of feelings. This will preclude the possibility of understanding. So sensitization

---

[1] Wilhelm Reich, *Character Analysis* (New York: Simon & Schuster, 1972), 338–339.

of the body is required via the dissolution of muscular armor and its tension patterns.

But the sensitization of the body is not just for the awareness of sensations and feelings. These are the first to be encountered by the expanding awareness. But the sensitivity, in time, needs to get deeper, and the perceptions need to get finer so that the organism can be aware of the subtler presence of essence itself. Essence is an embodied existence and will be experienced in the body, not somewhere else or abstractly.

When some authors write of the refinement of perception, there is more intended than to make the mind sharper and the body more feeling. By awakening the body and refining its sensitivity, the deeper and subtler capacities of perception are awakened and developed. These subtle capacities are organized by the subtle energetic centers, which are to be found in various locations in the body. And these subtle capacities for perception are needed for awareness of essential presence.

Essence, as we have seen, is a subtle substance that has physical characteristics. This means that in order to experience essence the physical organism has to become sensitive enough to perceive these physical characteristics, which are usually coexistent with the ordinary physical sensations. The physical characteristics of essential substance are very subtle, in the sense that they are quiet and silent compared to the sensations of the body and its feelings. Usually, they are drowned by the grosser sensations. They might be present, but because the person is attuned only to the grosser, more familiar physical sensations, he might not be aware of their presence. So his awareness will have to become refined enough to be sensitive to the subtler and finer sensations of essence.

The capacity to sense oneself must become so refined that the individual can discriminate between physical sensation and the sensation of essential substance. It is not enough that the mind be quiet. It is also necessary for the body to be sensitive. The mind can be quiet while the body is deadened. The body has to be awakened so that the center of sensing, the belly center, can be activated. The belly center, or what Gurdjieff called the physical center, is the center of sensing for all parts of the body. Its deepest function is the subtle sensing, the sensing of essential presence, that the Sufis call the organ for touch.

Touch is, in a sense, the most intimate of the physical senses. The skin must be directly against an object to touch it. There is no intermediary medium, like sound for hearing or light for seeing. So this subtle capacity is a very intimate one. Accurately speaking, it is sensing essence by being essence. It is the most direct way of perception. This capacity of touch, connected with the belly center, is very intimately connected with the embodiment of essence. It is the body center; its mode of perception is embodiment. Here, perception as touch, and being, are the same act. So this capacity is the most important one.

Also, touch gives us information about the physical characteristics of texture, density, temperature, viscosity, and the like. The term *touch* is used because, in fact, it is more accurate than the term *sensing* when it comes to essential experience. Sensing is used by the ordinary person to gain information about feelings and sensations. These usually do not have characteristics of texture, density, and viscosity. But essence does have these characteristics because it is a substance, although it is in a subtle dimension.

We can see very clearly that refinement of perception cannot be restricted to the mental. The mind, as we ordinarily understand it, cannot reach essence. The body must be sensitized so that the subtle organs of perception can be awakened.

Sensitizing the body will also awaken the capacity for taste, centered in the heart in the chest. "The heart (qalb) is the organ which produces true knowledge. . . . It is the organ of a perception which is both experience and intimate taste (dhowq)."[2]

This organ of perception (*dhowq*) is different and distinct from the organ of sensing, although it operates similarly to it. Just like the tongue, it can touch, and it also tastes in the same act of touching. It gives us information about the important physical characteristic of taste, needed for the appreciation of the essence and the fulfillment of the heart. The popular feeling that love is sweet is based on the essential aspect of love, which has a sweet taste. There are many kinds of love on the essential dimension, and each has its distinct sweetness. This capacity for inner taste is important also for appreciation and enjoyment, for discriminating and understanding the

---

[2] Henry Corbin, *Creative Imagination in the Sufism of Ibn 'Arabi*, trans. Ralph Manheim, Bollingen Series 91. Copyright © 1969 by Princeton University Press. Excerpt, p. 221.

various kinds of love, and for the other essential aspects, which also have different kinds of tastes.

Speaking of the "flavor" of an idea, situation, or perception is probably based on the reality of inner taste. Essence literally has a flavor. When we refer to subtle perceptions of essence as taste, we are not only speaking metaphorically. The metaphor is valid, but the literal and actual reality exists as well.

The third major capacity for subtle perception is that of seeing, connected with the head center in the forehead. This capacity provides information about color and shape, so necessary for understanding essence, for discriminating the various aspects, and for the aesthetic appreciation of the beauty of essence.

The popular expression "I see," meaning "I understand," is probably rooted in the fact of this capacity for perception. Here seeing is tantamount to understanding. The capacity for subtle seeing can be developed to the point of being freed from limitations of space and time. One can see inside the body, can see the anatomical parts of the body, even the cells and the molecules; one can see the emotions, the subtle energies, the essence. One can see things at a distance or in other times.

There are other capacities for subtle perception, such as smelling and hearing, but here we are giving examples only for general illustration. Connecting these various capacities with different energetic centers does not mean that it is only in those locations that the capacities are exercised. In fact, such capacities can be exercised, when developed, at any location in the body; indeed, they overlap. Texture can be discriminated by taste, even by seeing, as can density and viscosity. This is also true for the physical senses. However, here the phenomenon points to a very deep truth, that of the unity of senses, or capacities of perception. At the deeper dimension of essence, the centers lose their importance. They are important only at the start, as points of orientation or origination. Later, we see that these capacities are part of the essence itself, that essence itself has the capacity for touch, taste, seeing, hearing, smelling, intuition, knowing, and so on. In other words, the essence *is* the organ of perception. On this level of realization, all of the capacities are one capacity. It is one act of essence. It is possible to say that essence is consciousness, pure consciousness.

A deep characteristic of essence is that the deeper the realization, the more unification there is in the experience. At some point, even the capacities for perception are unified. The essence is self-aware. It knows itself, intuits itself, sees itself, hears itself, smells itself, tastes itself, touches itself. But all this is in one act, one unified perception. Of course, there is no separation between subject and object in this self-awareness. Essence is itself the consciousness.

The discrimination between the capacities, which happens at a different level of experience, is, so to speak, a result of analysis of the one capacity, the one sensitivity. The body, with its subtle physiology, acts like a prism on the basic sensitivity. This analysis and discrimination is needed for specialization at other levels of functioning.

The Sequence of Development

As awareness expands and sensitivity deepens, the individual undergoes successive experiences and transformations that necessitate dealing with various sectors of the personality and the life situations connected to them. There is a general sequence of inner events that will transform the person. In the Diamond Approach, this sequence is not rigid, and students often do not follow it exactly. Since the Approach works with the personality, there are many variations in sequence because personality differs in character, type, rigidity, level of organization, and history, from one person to another. The point of beginning can differ, and the sequence itself can differ. This characteristic of the Approach has the advantage of being geared to individual needs and situations instead of being a technique that has to be applied to all, the same way, regardless of character or extent of development. Each student works specifically with the material he comes with: his own personality, his actual life, at the time he starts the journey. This contributes to efficiency and economy in time and energy. This characteristic of the Approach also guards it from becoming a mechanical device that can be applied without understanding. Mechanicalness robs any method of the life element and in time renders it useless.

Still, there is a general sequence of events and realizations that people generally follow spontaneously. There are primary and universal signposts. The variations exist within an overall pattern. This pattern is dictated by the basic general structure of personality. The work starts from the surface layers of the personality and moves deeper and deeper. The structure of the personality determines the sequence of inner experiences and transformations. Because most people have a similar general structure, the developmental work follows a general sequence.

Important deviations from this general sequence are connected to deviated structures of the personality—structural deficiencies or distortions. For instance, a strongly borderline structure will begin essential unfoldment with an aspect of essence that the normal structure will not experience until after a long term of development. So in our discussion of sequence we are referring mostly to the normal structure, a structure with a well-developed ego and a cohesive sense of self.

One way of seeing this sequence is through the structural model of the personality introduced first by Sigmund Freud. The structure of the personality, which he called the psychic apparatus, consists of three structural units, arranged hierarchically; namely, the id, ego, and superego.

The id forms the instinctual, mostly psychophysiological basis of the whole structure. The ego, which is mostly based on the id, is the part that comes in contact with the external world. It is formed by the process of contact with and adaptation to the environment, mostly the parents. The superego is a structure that forms the apex of the psychic structure and includes the ideals of the personality and the principles of judgment. It is the seat of what is customarily called the conscience. It develops mainly by internalizing and identifying with the prohibitions, rules, values, and preferences of the parents and society at large.

The sequence of development in the Diamond Approach follows the line of regression of this structure. The part last formed and organized, the superego, becomes the first part the individual deals with and understands. Then the ego becomes the focus, and finally the id itself with its instincts and drives.

As we have already stated, this is the sequence of development that usually occurs for the normal person or the mildly neurotic person. For the severely neurotic person or the individual with character disorders, such as the borderline syndromes, the narcissistic personality disorders, and the psychoses, there is generally no such sequence because in the severe pathologies, the structure of the personality itself is distorted and flawed.

This does not mean that people with severe pathologies are candidates for the work of inner development. They are not, except under very special circumstances. They are in need of something else: the development of a well-functioning structure. It is only theoretically possible at this point that the Diamond Approach be used for such people, using the presence of essence to develop a balanced and well-functioning structure. This possibility is still in the stage of investigation, and no definite conclusions can be drawn yet.

However, even neurotic and normal personalities have features similar to these severe pathologies. Sometimes the difference is only in the degree of pathology. The extent of the presence of borderline, narcissistic, and psychotic features in neurotic and normal personality structures is just beginning to be acknowledged in psychological circles. It is still very far from being seen objectively.

From our perspective, everybody has neurotic, borderline, narcissistic, and psychotic features in his personality, each stemming from its developmental anlage in the process of ego development. People differ in the preponderance and intensity of the different developmental features in their personalities. Diagnosis in terms of neurotic, borderline, and so on is useful only for the practical purposes of applying technique and judging what is the best sequence of development for a particular student. For instance, a normal person with borderline tendencies might need to deal to some extent with some of the features of his ego structure before it is possible or even desirable to deal effectively with his superego.

The Superego

We will discuss briefly, and very generally, the salient features of the sequence of development in the case of the normal person. We will leave the more precise description for future publications. The deepest and most direct truths will have to be left to the oral transmission, to the process of teaching itself.

As awareness expands, the person becomes aware first of the necessity to find ways of dealing with his superego. This is the first important task. Without this ability, the individual will find it extremely difficult to expand his awareness and deal with his unconscious.

The reason is that the status quo of the personality is maintained by the superego. In particular, the status quo is continued by keeping the unconscious unconscious, by enforcing the defensive mechanisms of the ego. The agent that enforces these defensive functions is the superego.

We need to understand the process of repression in order to understand this mechanism more fully: awareness of unconscious material causes anxiety to the ego. The ego responds to anxiety with repression; it cuts off awareness from the arising unconscious material. In this way it avoids experiencing the anxiety and thus avoids the disintegrating effect of the anxiety on the ego structure.

Originally, the anxiety was the fear of the coercive agencies in childhood, mostly represented by the parents. Whenever the parents disapprove of a certain action or feeling of the child—and this happens repeatedly—the child learns, out of fear of this disapproval and also out of love for the parents, to suppress and finally repress this particular action or feeling. However, the disapproval becomes internalized in time as part of the child's own superego. So eventually, whenever a situation provokes this particular action or emotional state, the child's own superego disapproves and, in fact, punishes the child with guilt, shame, and other painful affects. The fear becomes a fear of one's own superego. The child, out of this fear of the superego and the punishment, learns to defend himself the way he did with his parents. He represses the particular action or feeling. He cuts off his awareness from his own impulses, feelings, and actions. For this to be effective, the whole operation must become unconscious and automatic. The unconscious remains unconscious out of fear of the superego and to defend against its attacks. Thus, the superego becomes the inner coercive agency that guards the status quo of the personality.

This means that in developing awareness and becoming aware of some parts of the unconscious, the individual will run into the fear of the superego and into its painful attacks themselves if he goes beyond the fear. Besides causing much pain and suffering, this confrontation with the superego will inhibit awareness and its expansion unless the person finds a solution for this situation. Psychoanalysis deals with this situation by analyzing it and understanding its genesis. In time, this process ameliorates the situation. The superego becomes more realistic in its demands and standards, and its attacks become gentler. Other schools use different methods to deal with the superego directly or indirectly, but all psychotherapeutic methods work only to ameliorate the situation. The superego continues to be an important and active part of the personality. The possibility of the complete dissolution of the superego is not envisioned in psychotherapy nor is it seen as a desirable end.

This is obviously because the *Weltanschauung*, the world view of the analyst and the psychotherapist, does not include the fact of essence. The presence of essence, with its direct and objective perception and its balanced human nature, is not known, so the possibility of a life without the superego but instead with such an objective perception is not envisioned. The capacity of the essence to know and to act according to knowledge is not seen. So there remains always the belief in the need for ideals, morals, and rules to govern one's life. From our perspective, the superego is the inner coercive agency that stands against the expansion of awareness and inner development, regardless of how mild or reasonable it becomes. It is a substitute, and a cruel one, for direct perception and knowledge. Inner development requires that in time there be no internal coercive agencies. There will be instead inner regulation based on objective perception, understanding, and love.

The best approach is to decrease the power and influence of the superego and to replace it with awareness as much as possible, all the way to the final and complete dethronement of the superego. This establishes, in turn, some important aspects of essence.

The ego automatically and unconsciously responds to the superego with repression of parts of the personality, to defend itself against its painful attacks. An effective way to deal with the superego is to learn to defend against its attacks in a different way, without having to use repression and the other unconscious defense mechanisms of the ego.[3] The method has to be conscious and intentional,

---

[3] Anna Freud, *The Ego and Its Mechanism of Defense* (London: Hogarth Press), 1937.

in contrast to the habitual automatic ways that can only foster unconsciousness. Learning how to defend consciously and intentionally against the superego and its attacks is learning a whole understanding and a whole inner technology.[4] It is taking into consideration the understanding of what the superego is and using one's own intelligence to deal with it and defend against its attacks.

Let's take a simple example to illustrate this method. Let's suppose a man feels ashamed every time he feels tenderness toward another person. The superego attacks him with shame and belittling, according to the judgment that tenderness in a man means he is weak and feminine. To begin work on his superego, first the man needs to be aware of the attack, its content, and the content of the judgment. Then he needs to understand the judgment psychodynamically. For instance, he might remember that his father had the attitude that men should be tough, that tenderness belongs to girls and women. Here he understands that he introjected his father's attitude and made it part of his superego. He usually responds to this attitude, which is an attack on himself, with shame and repression. Now, in applying this method, he envisions his father and tells him, in his mind: "Daddy, go to hell! Who cares what you think of me?" Here he is dealing with his superego in a way he could not have dealt with his father in his childhood. He was not able to defend against his father because he believed him, was scared of him, and needed him. This method might not work the first time, but if it is done repeatedly, it will bring out the man's aggression, and he will be able to assert himself and separate from his father's attitude.

The defense needs to be intelligent to be effective. For instance, if the man responds with: "Father, it's not true I am feminine and weak. Tenderness is good and does not mean weakness or femininity," then he is being reasonable with a superego that is not really rational. Also, he probably has tried this response many times but without success because in this response the man is on the defensive; he is trying to justify his feeling and to account to somebody else for its being okay. Any justification already implies some guilt, and so it won't work. The response of "Daddy, go to hell" is effective because there is no attempt at explanation or justification and thus no im-

---

[4] Henry Korman, personal communication.

plication of unconscious guilt. The man just throws back the attack and refuses to listen to its content. He completely disengages from the superego and does not give it any power over him.

It is difficult to appreciate the power and effectiveness of this method, without learning it and trying it for some time. But when a person does learn to defend against his superego, in time he will not need to use the unconscious defense mechanisms. Then a little work on paying attention will bring out the unconscious material. This is a gradual process of opening the unconscious, which is of paramount importance for inner development. The individual learns to become so skilled and facile in dealing with the superego that the superego gradually loses its grip. The structure of the superego itself becomes exposed for understanding, which helps to dissolve its structural basis.

This method, if applied all the way, will lead to the realization and development of several essential aspects. The activation of aggression for defense and assertion leads to the essential aspect of strength. In time it will lead to the essential aspect of the self, the true identity. The intelligence needed for this method develops in time into the essential aspect of objective consciousness, the diamond body. The moral rules and standards of judgment in time give way to essential conscience. This aspect of essence becomes the true protector of essence, the real defense, replacing the unconscious defense mechanisms of the ego.

However, working toward that level of realization will lead to working on the ego and the id, the deeper determinants of the structure of the superego.

THE CHAKRAS

The work on the superego, on expanding the awareness and deepening the sensitivity of the body, involves the activation and freeing the chakra level of energetic functioning. This does not necessarily mean direct work on the physical location of the chakras. It is basically clearing the mind and opening the body, which inevitably involves the clearing of the chakra system. The chakra system is basically the level of emotions, thinking processes, and physiological functioning. Freeing these functions from the unconscious, defending against the superego, and clearing the conflicts in the mind, is itself the work on clearing the chakras.

Of course, there are other methods of dealing with this level of work. Some systems work directly on the chakra system and its centers. Others activate the kundalini energy and use it to activate and clear the chakras. Others use yogic physical techniques. Psychotherapy and the body therapies also are attempts in this direction.

The chakras do not function properly because of the body armor and its patterns of psychophysical tensions. The work on the superego, especially if coupled with somatic-energetic techniques, such as those that employ breathing, is a powerful and efficient method for clearing this level. It also guards against the fascination and the excitement characteristic of direct work on the chakras.

Clearing this level of the personality leads at some point to the regaining of the pure emotional energy, and culminates in the experience of the void.

THE VOID

The work on the superego ultimately will expose one of its cornerstones: castration anxiety. Freud established that the superego is based mainly on the castration complex. He explained that for the child to resolve his castration fear he develops and strengthens his identification with the parent of the same sex. In particular, the child identifies with the parent's prohibiting and admonishing attitudes, and this is the main identification that builds the structure of the superego. There are deeper bases for the superego's structure, originating in the symbiotic stage of ego development, but we are now dealing only with the selective identifications that occur during the oedipal period and that form the major structure of the superego.

By learning to defend consciously against the superego, the individual is really rejecting, or rather separating from, this identification with the parent of the same sex, which will ultimately bring out to consciousness the basis of the identification. Since the identifications relevant here are with the parent of the same sex, they include a sexual identification. Dealing with this identification and the deeper castration complex is tantamount, in the Diamond Approach, to dealing with a certain specific hole in the personality. This hole is related to a distortion in self-image, particularly in the genital part of the body image. The castration complex is itself the main cause of this distortion; this is true for both sexes.

So we see that dealing with the superego will at some point expose the identifications that repress the castration complex. Dealing with this issue brings out the specific hole connected with castration, which is a distortion in the body image aspect of the self-image. The hole or deficiency is simply an unconscious body image of having no genitals or no sexuality. Accepting and understanding this feeling and belief of deficiency will bring forth its corresponding essential aspect, which turns out to be the void (space). This essential aspect is the correction of the distortion in the body image. This distortion is really a distortion of space. The void is the experience of oneself, one's essence, as empty space. It is an experience of expansion, spaciousness, openness, and boundlessness. The mind is not bound by the rigid boundaries of the personality's self-image. Its effect on perception is to see things as they are, without distortion. The experience of the genital hole is a distortion of how things are because there is really no hole there. The emerging space erases this distortion.

The void is really nothing but the absence of the personality and its various distortions. The mind is empty then, completely empty of the personality. It is as if the inner space is cleaned out, emptied, of the personality and its patterns, mental or physical. The person feels free, fresh, light, and unhampered. The mind is seen as it is, an immaculate emptiness.

THE LATAIF

This experience of space heralds the process of essential realization and development. There is room now for something other than the world of the personality. Before this realization, the personality filled everything. There was no space for essence.

It is this experience that many people call ego death, contending that it is necessary for the birth of essence. In reality, it is the beginning of ego death. The personality must go through many transformations, called deaths, before it relinquishes its hold. But this experience of space does lead to the rebirth, the emergence of essence.

This condition of openness and spaciousness usually leads, by itself, to the activation of the centers of the subtle physiology, called the lataif. We let the foremost representative of Sufism in the West, Seyyid Idries Shah, discuss the lataif: "The human being is stated, in Sufi representation, to contain five elements of the 'relative' and five of the 'absolute' . . . . There are said to be five centers of spiritual perception, corresponding to these ranges of experience. They are conceived of as having physical locations in the human body."[5]

Most Sufi writers agree that there are five primary lataif, or centers of perception, and there is a general agreement about the colors associated with them and their localizations in the human body.

The one at the left side of the body is usually called *qalb*, meaning "heart." The color yellow is associated with it. The state of consciousness here is that of true joy and delight in which essence exists in the condition of unadulterated joy. Its activation and realization also are connected with the transformation of a certain sector of the personality, a process that is sometimes referred to as the yellow death.

The latifa on the right side of the body is usually called *rouh*, meaning "spirit" or "soul." The color is red, and the consciousness is of true and real strength. It is like the fire of essence and requires the transformation of the personality referred to as the red death, or the freedom from fear of people.

The third latifa is located at the solar plexus and is associated with the color white, or silver. The consciousness is that of true will, which is the support for essence and its life. The white death is the transformation of the personality relevant here, which is death into God. The name of this latifa is *sirr*, which means "secret." In fact, the activation of this center is seen often as the initial step or the transition from the world of the personality to the dimension of essence.

---

[5] Idries Shah, *A Perfumed Scorpion* (London: Octagon Press, 1978), 89–90.

The fourth latifa is at the forehead between and just above the eyebrows. It is called *khafi*, meaning "hidden," and the color is a shining black. The consciousness is a state of peace and absolute stillness, related to the activity of intuition and objective understanding. It is connected to the black death, which is the state of annihilation of the sense of identity of the ego, which is the false self.

The fifth latifa is at the center of the chest, called *akhfa*, meaning "more hidden," and the color is emerald green. The consciousness is that of loving-kindness and compassion. The Sufis take this latifa to be the most central and most important. This is understandable for many reasons. Compassion is selflessness and is equated with selfless action. This latifa also leads to the nature of the heart, which is the essential aspect of absolute truth. Also, this center is connected to the essential aspect that is referred to in the literature as the pearl beyond price, which is the personal being.

The lataif, as Shah says, are not only centers but also forms of consciousness, operating on the subtle dimension. These forms of consciousness when understood precisely, will be seen as a dimension of essence, a subtle form of substance. They comprise the subtle body (*Jism latif*). They are the beginning experience of essence in some of its basic aspects. For instance, the green latifa is the beginning of compassion, or the loving kindness aspect of essence. The red latifa is the beginning of the strength aspect of essence, and so on.

They are called lataif, meaning qualities that have subtlety, gentleness, and refinement to them, and are the first subtle and fine manifestation of essence. To use an analogy: if essence is like the oil of a perfume, the lataif will be its aromas. A latifa is like the vapor of the oil, which, in turn, is the essential substance. So the lataif are forms of essence that is a fine, very subtle, and gentle presence that pervades space. It is so fine and so subtle that it is very likely that an individual will fail to discriminate it from space, the void.

Of course, as each latifa is activated, it will bring out with it to consciousness a certain sector of the personality, which must be confronted and understood objectively. The experience of the void does not indicate that the work on the personality has ended, definitely not. It heralds the *beginning* of essential development.

We say here that space leads to the activation of the lataif, which is the beginning of essential realization. But the process does not always occur in this sequence. This sequence is the natural one, and many systems, such as Buddhism, take it into consideration in their methods. The Buddhist counterpart to the realm of the lataif is what is called the realm of the five Dhyani-Buddhas, the peaceful deities of the *Tibetan Book of the Dead.*

> At the center of all bardo visions stand the five Tathāgastas (TrGyal-ba rigs Inga). They form a first pentad in Buddhist mandala, and in their comprehensive multiplicity of meaning they constitute a many-leveled background for the development of most of the esoteric teachings of Vajrayāna Buddhism. For the various versions of the Tibetan Book of the Dead, which has its own tradition, they are the essence and the foundation for statements about the nature of man and his psychological structure, and they are at the same time the primordial images for the spiritual path to transcendence and liberation. The doctrine of the five Tathagatas concerns possibilities of clarification of awareness in this earthly life as well as the possibility of attaining the illuminated path of wisdom of the Buddhas in the bardo.[6]

The Dhyani-Buddhas (Tathagatas) do not coincide exactly with the five lataif; the Buddhist system has the consciousness connected to the color blue, instead of the black of the Sufis.

Other work systems, like the Sufi one, do not follow this sequence and attempt to activate the lataif directly. This occurs sometimes in the Diamond Approach if the person happens to be working on the particular personality segment connected with one of the lataif. Working on this segment all the way can lead to the related hole, which will activate the connected latifa and its particular subtle essence. This can happen before the discovery of space, but it is not the norm.

Other methods attempt first, through certain techniques plus interactions of teacher with student, to bring out the essential substance. Then the essential substance is used to activate the lataif. The activation of the lataif will, in turn, transsubstantiate the essence,

---

[6] Detlef Ingo Lauf, *Secret Doctrines of the Tibetan Book of the Dead* (Boulder, CO, and London: Shambhala, 1977), 104–105.

that is, transform the essential substance into the various aspects and dimensions.

However, space must be realized at some point; otherwise the personality will come back and clamp down strongly against the emerging essence. This will make it difficult for the essence to be present permanently, and techniques and practices will have to be employed all the time in order to stay in touch with it. The Sufi method of *Dhikr* (remembrance) and the tantric method of mantra (chanting) are some of these methods that must be done continually to remember essence and keep present.

THE ESSENCE

The work on developing the lataif then continues by understanding the emerging sectors of the personality. Each one of the lataif has a sector of the personality connected to it that acts as a substitute for it and has the memory of the situations that led to its burial. All of these phenomena must be understood, precisely and exactly, for the centers to be permanently active.

Each of the subtle forms of the consciousness is then understood, experienced, and embodied. The effects of the lataif on the person's consciousness are understood and integrated. This has a permanent influence on the personality; the personality is in fact transformed by accommodating the impact of the lataif on its structure and consciousness.

Beyond that, each of the lataif functions, so to speak, as a door or entry into a whole universe, a whole dimension of essence. Each is an entry into a realm of the being that has in it many essential aspects. For instance, the yellow latifa leads to the essential aspects of pleasure, fulfillment, satisfaction, contentment, and various forms of love.

The situation can be looked at either as each of the lataif developing and expanding into deeper and deeper dimensions of essence, or as each of the lataif as a door leading into different realms of essence. Experientially, the two points of view are the same.

As we have said, the relation of the lataif to essence is like the perfume to the oil of the perfume. By following the scent, the perfume, we will be led to the substance of the perfume—the concentrated perfume, the essence—provided we have a good nose, that is, well-developed capacities of perception.

The process is like the one we described in Chapter Four in the example of the merging essence. Psychological constellations will present themselves both inside—as emotional conflicts and physical tension—and outside—as difficulties, conflicts, issues, dissatisfactions, and lack of understanding of the environment and the people in it. Since at this stage it is easy to deal with the superego, now the unconscious material is more available. The teacher will be able to see the large patterns, the specific psychological constellations that form sectors of the personality, each related to an essential aspect. This will help the student to focus more on the real issues and to be more precise in his observations.

The psychological constellation, when understood exactly for what it is, will lead spontaneously to a related hole of the personality, which the individual will experience emotionally as a certain lack or deficiency, usually defended against by various antics. Acceptance of this hole leads to experiencing the personality as an emptiness. This emptiness, this void, is like a death for the personality. It is actually a death of the particular sector of the personality but is experienced psychologically as an overall death of the personality.

When this "death" is completely understood and accepted, the corresponding aspect of essence emerges and fills the emptiness left by the personality. The essential aspect that emerges will be exactly what was lacking and will be precisely what the individual has been attempting to get from the outside, through the related personality patterns. The exactness, the fitness, is usually difficult to believe. It is completely precise. The individual realizes that he had known unconsciously exactly what he was missing and that his thoughts, emotions, and actions were motivated by this unconscious knowing, without his even suspecting it. The experience can be termed "mind-blowing." It is usually, however, a quiet and peaceful experience, mostly invisible to the outside observer; but its exactness and its meaningfulness are staggering.

This emergence of essence is what is usually referred to in Work literature as a "rebirth." The essence is born again, having been buried for years. The birth is a completion of a cycle, preceding the beginning of another cycle. The whole process repeats itself; understanding a new constellation or sector of the personality leads to its specific deficient hole (emptiness) and ends with the emergence of the corresponding essential aspect. There is awakening, death, and rebirth for each aspect of the essence—awakening to a certain sector of the personality, the death of this sector in the experience of emptiness, and then the rebirth as the emerging of the aspect of essence. This cycle is repeated as many times as there are holes in the personality.

As we see, there is no one death and no one rebirth, unless we take the first emergence of essence as the unitary experience. The personality dies gradually, one sector at a time. We see here the meaning of the cycle of death and rebirth. This sequence of awakening, death, and rebirth is the usual one known from ancient times, but here it is seen with diamond clarity. Gurdjieff puts it this way:

> "When a man awakes he can die; when he dies he can be born."
> We must find out what this means.
> "To awake," "to die," "to be born." These are three successive stages. If you study the Gospels attentively you will see that references are often made to the possibility of being born, several references are made to the necessity of "dying," and there are very many references to the necessity of "awakening"—"watch, for you know not the day and the hour . . ." and so on.[7]

The Diamond Approach adds precision and lawfulness to this process. This precision is responsible for the effectiveness and efficiency of the Diamond Approach. The vague, metaphoric, or poetic ways of describing the process of rebirth often add more confusion than clarification. The metaphoric and poetic formulations are aesthetically appealing and often powerfully inspiring, but for a person who is thirsting—even dying—a beautiful way of describing the road that leads to the well is not as important as a clear, precise, and succinct way. Also, the precision has an aesthetic of its own, a clear and luminous beauty like the beauty of a precious diamond.

---

[7] P. D. Ouspensky, *In Search of the Miraculous* (New York: Harcourt, Brace & World, 1949), 217. Used by permission.

ESSENTIAL ASPECTS

We have said that essence has various aspects that are unique and distinct from each other. They are all essence, all substantial, but different in qualitative experience, function, and influence on the personality. It is as if they are different organs of the same organism, and this organism is one's being. They are all necessary, and the being is incomplete without any one of them.

Also, these aspects are absolute. They are absolute in the sense that they cannot be reduced further to something else or analyzed into simpler constituents. Love is love and is always love. And love is not the same as will. Will is always will, although it is essence, just as love is essence. These absolute aspects of essence are reminiscent of the Platonic forms or ideas that Plato recorded from Socrates' arguments.

In fact, Socrates knew that these absolute forms of the human essence are within us, because he asserted and proved logically (for example, in Plato's *Meno*) that they cannot be learned. He thought that a person can only remember them, that nobody can learn them from somebody else or through deduction or experience. A person can know them only by remembering them.

This is a deep truth that Socrates knew without having the knowledge about the personality that is available to us now. Now we understand his philosophy psychodynamically; we understand psychologically why we can only remember essence states.

We saw in Chapter Three, in our discussion of the theory of holes, that a hole gets filled by a sector of the personality that is related to the lost aspect of essence. We also saw that this sector of the personality is related to its particular aspect of essence by the unconscious memories of the experiences and situations that led to the loss and of the emotions involved in those experiences. In fact, this sector of the personality has in it the memory of the essential aspect itself, and so it is intimately connected to this aspect of essence. Its beginning and development contain the memory of the lost aspect, but the memory is mostly repressed. To remember it consciously involves confronting the painful situations that instituted the repression.

So Socrates is right. Essential aspects or absolute forms can be known only by being remembered, by being dredged up from the deepest recesses of the unconscious and experienced consciously. We have not shown, however, that it cannot be known in a different way, such as from somebody else (the way math is learned, for example.) We won't attempt this. However, it is enough for our purposes to point out that essence is a category of experience not accessible to the logical, "mental" mind. It cannot be communicated by the mind to somebody else. Most teachers, in fact, stress that essence is found inside, that the teacher can only point to it, or at best can ignite the inner flame with his own. But the flame is one's own and can be known only directly, within oneself, by oneself.

That the personality has the memory of the lost essence somewhere in its unconscious is evident in the manifestations of the personality in its patterns, dreams, and hopes. We saw this in the last chapter, with respect to the merging essence, in the desire of the personality for the experience of merging with somebody else when all boundaries of the personality are melted away. We see the movement toward the lost merging essence in the desire for closeness, community, or physical contact, just to mention a few.

An object relations psychologist might object to this assertion by saying that the individual is not remembering the merging love of essence but is rather remembering the symbiotic relationship with the mother. It is true that the individual is remembering the symbiotic relationship, the dual unity, in this instance; but this does not explain all the facts. It does not explain the utterances and the fantasies, many of which seem not to involve the mother, that some people have when they are deeply feeling this desire. It does not explain why they think this desired contact is sweet, that it has a melting quality to it, that it has a golden glow—all characteristics of the merging essence. It does not explain why some people have the fantasy of entering a golden womb or being drowned in a golden puddle when they experience the symbiotic wish.

More thorough documentation, including case histories, will be presented in future publications. It is enough for us now to have some inkling of the truth that the personality has the memory, albeit unconscious, of essence and its aspects.

The personality not only has the memory of the essential aspects but in fact uses this unconscious memory in its attempt to fill the particular hole, by filling it with a fake quality or with hopes of getting it from outside. The final picture is that this sector of the personality takes the place of the essential aspect. It acts as a substitute for it. The servant of the house behaves after a while as the master of the house.

All sectors of the personality, all qualities of the personality, all characteristics of the personality are substitutes for the essential ones. The personality, in fact, is an exact replica of the essence, but it is false. It is made up, a reaction, an outcome, and does not have the reality of essence. It is a plastic substitute that lacks the aliveness, freshness, realness, and luminous clarity of the real thing.

This is a painful and difficult situation, but in this situation resides the key to its resolution. Because all sectors of the personality are substitutes for and imitations of the aspects of essence, they are really faithful pointers to these aspects. By understanding these sectors we can regain the aspects of essence. Instead of condemning the personality, as most work systems do, we can use it as a guide and a faithful guide at that. The personality contains the keys to its own riddles. Some of the ancient schools realized this fact, and employed it in their work.

This understanding is of a great help in the journey of return. The personality is seen not only as the barrier but also as containing the keys. It brings out in the student an attitude of acceptance, compassion, and a genuine desire to understand the truth of the personality. This is exactly the attitude needed for doing the work of inner development.

Let's use a simple example to illustrate this point. Let's take one of the deepest characteristics of the personality, greed. This quality of wanting more and more, of never having enough, has always been observed in the personality and has been criticized and condemned by almost all systems and teachers. Greed has generally been viewed from a materialistic perspective and not much attempt has been made to understand it objectively.

Let's apply to this example our perspective that each characteristic of the personality is a false substitute for a characteristic of the essence. The personality usually wants what the essence is, but sees it as outside and also sees it in a distorted way. We saw these factors in our discussion of the merging essence. The personality wants to get the merging essence from outside and imagines it as some kind of a completely fulfilling contact with another being. But the resolution of this desire is an aspect of essence that exists inside us, as us.

Greed is wanting more and more from outside. Also, greed is not the desire for something in particular; it is a characteristic of insatiable desire. So it must be a reflection of a characteristic of essence per se and not of a particular essential aspect. It must function as an attempt to fill the hole, the deficiency resulting from the loss of this characteristic of essence.

The characteristic of essence that is connected to greed in the personality has a sense of "more and more," of limitlessness and endlessness. In fact, this quality of endlessness is a profound characteristic of essence. Each aspect of essence exists in an unlimited way or extent. The substance of essence is not limited in extent; it is infinite, limitless. In other words, we can say that each aspect of essence is really a boundless ocean of this quality. Merging essence, for example, does not exist in a certain amount. When the individual is open to this aspect, he is in fact connected to a limitless ocean of merging essence, to a whole infinite dimension of this sweet quality.

The personality has a memory of the endlessness of essence and its inexhaustability. But this abundance is projected outward, and then the personality wants more and more from the outside. So the hole filled by greed is the hole (deficiency) resulting from the loss of the characteristic of essence of abundance and infinity. In this characteristic of greed we find the pointer to the expansion, endlessness, and inexhaustability of essence. The personality wants what was lost, and what was lost is endless. The personality is not going to be stopped by moralistically accusing it of being greedy. It knows better. Its knowledge is deep. The characteristic of greed will not disappear unless its hole is experienced and filled with the actual abundance of essence.

There is another kind of greed, a greed for variety, of wanting many things, more and more things, all different. "I want this, and this, and that, and that, this one too; how about that one and that one. . . ." We see this quality of greed with children most clearly and straightforwardly.

But this characteristic of the personality reflects another characteristic of essence, which is the endlessness of its forms, aspects, characteristics, and dimensions. This is a deep truth of essence; essence has no end. There is no end of learning, no end of expansion. New qualities and aspects, new characteristics and different dimensions keep coming to the correctly oriented individual. The development keeps going; different dimensions, different qualities, different realms. Each one of them, in turn, goes through a development, an expansion. The process is limitless, endless, in all its sides and dimensions. Every time an individual believes he reached the end, a whole new dimension opens up. Dimensions can emerge from unexpected angles; developments can go in any direction. The endlessness of essence is what Gurdjieff is referring to in his major book, *All and Everything*, when he gives God the title of "his endlessness."

It is important to see here that understanding greed is not sanctioning greed. For the work to be done effectively, greed has to be understood instead of being acted out. The individual must observe and understand this characteristic of the personality, until its hole is revealed, which will reveal the ignorance of the essential characteristic of endlessness. This will then bring out the perception and the realization of the infinite richness of essence. Here greed dies.

When we refer to the different aspects of essence we do not indicate that we are seeing essence from different perspectives or different points of view. It does not mean we are seeing the same reality under different conditions or that we are calling it different names. We actually mean different distinct aspects. They are all essence, but they are distinct in their qualities and influence. They are like the various organs of the body. They are all the body, but they are not the same. The heart is not the same as the brain, and both are different from a leg. But they are all parts of the body.

Seeing essence in its various aspects, seeing these aspects as different and distinct, and giving each one a specific name, can lead to some difficulties for the student. This discrimination of aspects, and naming them, in a sense concretizes them. This specificity and delineation can lead to a certain form of attachment. It becomes easy for the personality to be attached to some of these aspects. The individual might want to experience the same aspect over and over. He might try to hold onto it and become afraid of losing it. He might develop the attitude of hoarding, of collecting more and more substance, or collecting various kinds of aspects. Essence is then being treated like any material possession. In other words, the objectification of the aspects can and does lead to spiritual materialism. This materialism, this attachment can then strengthen, instead of weakening, the rigid grip of the personality. This is counter to what is needed for inner work, where the personality must learn to let go, especially of its attachments. In fact, the personality's basic characteristic is attachment, which is the main cause of suffering.

Systems that are aware of this fact are usually very cautious—in fact, paranoid—about the possibility of spiritual materialism. Essence is referred to very vaguely. The aspects are not mentioned nor even conceived of. The whole thing is left formless, vague, and even referred to as unknowable.

But the belief that experiencing and naming the aspects of essence must lead to spiritual materialism is not completely accurate. It reflects a lack of complete trust in the nature of essence. When we talk about essence as the elixir, as the agent of transformation, we mean it literally. It is what catalyzes the inner transformation. It is true that objectivizing the aspects can lead to attachment and spiritual materialism. But this is not a negative development. In fact, we can see it in a positive light.

As long as an individual can be attached, then nothing will stop him from being so. Trying to avoid this attachment, as some systems do, will only keep it and its possibility repressed, still living in the unconscious. The personality will find any object to be attached to, if it still needs to. So the best approach, if the individual is interested in pursuing the truth all the way, is to bring this attachment to the surface so that it can be observed, understood, and truly resolved.

Spiritual materialism is not avoided in the Diamond Approach. It is allowed to surface, to come out into the light of consciousness. Then the attachments are studied and understood like any other characteristics of the personality.

In fact, essence itself will make sure that this happens. Attachments to essence or to some of its aspects cannot be ignored, especially not in the Diamond Approach. This attachment will be revealed naturally as a contraction or a restriction. The purity of essence and the process of its expansion will expose it as such. The individual will not be able to be attached and still experience essence freely. Attachment is personality, and it will manifest as a conflict that leads to suffering. In fact the more essence is manifesting, the more this conflict will be obvious.

Essence will reveal the attachments. There will emerge specific essential aspects whose particular effect on the individual is to expose these attachments. There will also emerge other essential aspects that will give the understanding that will specifically lead to nonattachment, to the freedom from all attachments. In fact, the deepest essential aspects cannot be realized and freed without dealing with the issues of attachment and spiritual materialism.

We see here that essence includes all the safeguards needed for inner freedom. It is truly and genuinely the agent of transformation. Trusting essence has to be complete. No experience can be shied away from if there is this total trust. It is the trust that essence will act in the best way, the most intelligent way, and the most compassionate way. It will strengthen parts of our personality only to expose them, so that there will be only freedom, a genuine freedom that is based on truth, not on control.

States and Stations

The rebirth of an essential aspect is the beginning of its life. It does not yet mean that this aspect is completely established. In fact, the rebirth might just be an isolated experience that fills the heart with joy for some time and then disappears. Or the aspect might show up once in a while, under certain circumstances, but not every time it is actually needed. This means that this aspect of essence is not completely freed; it is not yet made one's own.

The appearance or the experience of essence can happen sometimes without the individual going through the inner work of understanding and without experiencing the deficiency. This happens in isolated instances and usually has no lasting effect on the personality. It also can happen if the individual is associating with another who embodies the essence. This is the customary situation of disciples with their teachers and guides. If the disciple is open enough or is capable of empathic identification with his or her teacher, or most likely when the disciple is able to merge with the consciousness of the teacher, he or she might at certain times experience essence in some of its aspects.

This is, in fact, one of the main methods of transmission used by many teachers. It is sometimes referred to as initiation. However, as we have already pointed out, this is an isolated instance and does not mean the disciple has made the essence his own yet. Usually, the personality comes back and clamps down on the new openness. This is expected, because if essence is activated, it will bring out from the unconscious all of the psychological material associated with it, the material that led to its loss. If the individual does not then deal with this material, it will just bury the essence again, as it did in the first place. This is why work systems that do not have a methodology of working through the unconscious aspects of the personality are inefficient, even though the teacher might know and even embody the essence.

The disciples come to the presence of the teacher or guru, merge with his consciousness, and experience the essence, but they cannot take it with them. They leave it with the teacher because it is still his. This usually leads to a condition of dependency on and idealization of the teacher, which is contrary to the whole point of inner development. Those teaching systems become supply sources: the kids come to their mother, nurse at her breast, then go away, to return when their bellies are empty. The kids never grow, because they do not have the means to learn how to nurse themselves.

Idries Shah relates a story in which a visitor asks a Sufi how come some countries are full of gurus and spiritual teachers when there are only a few Sufis who appear to be teaching. The Sufi answers: "India, for instance, is full of gurus and shrine worshippers, and public Sufis of real truth are more than rare because the gurus and their followers are at play and the Sufis are at work. Without Sufi work, humanity would die out."[8]

It is not easy to recognize or appreciate true essential work. It is not a matter of having ecstatic experiences, of seeing visions, and so on, although these events happen as part of the learning process. The work is more for an individual to be a true and real human adult, integrated on all levels from the most physical to the most sublime. The work is oriented toward reality, truth, objectivity, completeness, and so on, and these things are not usually visible to one without inner development. Experiences are not only for enjoyment but are to be digested as nutrition essential for a human being if he is to grow to be an actual complete adult.

---

[8] Idries Shah, *Thinkers of the East* (London: Jonathan Cape, 1971), 27.

The condition of having isolated experiences of an essential aspect is termed by the Sufis the stage of the *hal*; the experience is still a state. A state is contrasted with a station (*maqam*) when the essential aspect is made one's own, when it is attained by one's own efforts and established permanently by such efforts.

That an essential aspect has become a station does not mean it is always present. This condition exists after it is just established, but as other aspects emerge they will displace it. In this case, a station means that the aspect is permanently available; it is present whenever the situation requires it.

Even in using the Diamond Approach, activating the essential aspects by going through the death of the corresponding sectors of the personality does not necessarily make them into stations. In some instances it does, but usually more work is needed. Sometimes not all relevant parts of the personality are seen and understood. The emerging essence will expose them. Then the inner work is on understanding all the arising parts of the personality associated with this aspect and the effect of the essential aspect on them.

The work that leads to the activation of an essential aspect usually exposes the main conflict around that aspect. But then this central conflict has many kinds of ramifications, all kinds of connections to other parts of the personality, and might bring about other central conflicts of the personality, connected to other aspects of essence. For instance, in the example of the merging essence, we saw in Chapters Three and Four that the central conflict is around the symbiotic wish for the mother. But when the merging essence is activated, it might expose another conflict—between its presence and the aspect of will, for instance. An individual might find out that when he was a child he repeatedly lost the symbiotic contact with his mother every time he asserted his will. This conflict will have to be resolved; otherwise, the individual will not be able to experience his merging essence whenever he happens to be experiencing essential will. In another case, the merging essence might become repressed again because the symbiotic wish for the mother might activate the oedipal wish for her, which may still be repressed. There are usually several intertwined conflicts around a given emerging aspect of essence.

This process of turning a state into a station can be seen in a way that sheds a different light on it. The process is that of working on having the essence, in whatever aspect it happens to be, present in all of an individual's life situations. He might experience essence in a certain situation but find it difficult to be essentially present when he is in a different situation. It is time then to turn one's attention to that situation to understand what exactly is causing the difficulty. The individual will then confront his anxiety and attempt to understand the unconscious material causing it, until it becomes possible for essence to be present in this situation. A person does not usually need to look for these situations; they are usually presented to him by his own personality functioning in his life. The culmination of this process is that the individual will be able to embody the essential aspect in all relevant situations; it becomes a station.

This process of making possible the presence of essence in external situations goes along with a similar process of freeing the essence in the inner environment. The essential aspect may flow in certain locations of the body but not in others. This is an indication of more issues to be resolved regarding the particular essence. The work then is understanding and resolving these barriers and blocks in the body, until the essence flows into them unhindered.

Let's take again our example of the merging essence. The individual might realize that his experience of it is restricted to the chest only, that whenever this aspect is present it does not go beyond the boundaries of the chest. He might want to believe that it is a heart quality, and that is why it is always located in the chest. But essence cannot be restricted this way. To be completely established, any aspect must attain the freedom to be anywhere in the body.

The individual might notice, if he applies his attention, that the merging essence is blocked from going downward into the body, particularly into the pelvis. Usually the essence will spontaneously go to the blocked area and expose the repression in it related to the particular aspect. But the individual must be interested in seeing the truth, whatever it is, for the process to proceed. The individual might find out, for instance, that when the merging essence flows into the genital area it activates the wish for genital merging. This might bring out conflicts around sexuality, oedipal and otherwise. These conflicts need to be understood and resolved for the merging essence to exist freely in the genital area.

This process usually continues of its own accord if the individual is committed to the truth. The essence keeps extending its territory, displacing the personality, until it reclaims the totality of the body. Then the essence fills the whole body, the totality of the organism. Each cell is then full and vivified by the presence of essence. The whole organism is then unified and integrated.

This is a true experience of integration. It is not only that the individual experiences his body as a whole, as one unit, but he experiences himself, all of himself, as a unified, integrated, homogeneous presence. There are no barriers, no partitions inside. There are no parts experienced together, as integration is usually understood. On the essential dimension, integration is actual and literal. The individual experiences himself as one homogeneous medium, which is the substance of essence. It is truly being one.

Many people consider the experience of unity or integration as the experience of all the parts fitting together, working together, and in harmony with each other. This experience is still mechanical from the perspective of essence. When an essential aspect is completely integrated, when it is a station, then it is experienced as one homogeneous substance without partitions. Instead of parts integrated, it is like a pool of water. And the individual experiences himself as this pool—complete unification and true integration.

The Pearl Beyond Price

In the course of this chapter's discussion of essential development, the reader might have noted that the process has been more of uncovering buried aspects of essence than any actual development. This brings us to the issue of development versus uncovering.

Some systems have formulated the Work in terms of developing something that is already there, or even developing something that is not even there. Other systems have made their formulations in the form of uncovering and bringing out the essence that is already there and already formed but inaccessible to experience.

The systems of the first kind assume that essence is not there to start with, or is there in a primitive and undeveloped form that needs refinement and evolution. The second kind of system assumes the human organism has everything in it, already formed and complete and only needing to be exposed. In most circumstances this difference leads to a divergence of methods and techniques.

Another way of formulating the issue is to see development and uncovering as two complementary aspects of inner work, to assume that both are true. Sometimes they refer to the same and sometimes to different aspects or phases of inner work.

The way we have described the process so far appears as more of an uncovering. The essence is buried, and the work is to uncover it and make it conscious. Even the work on stations does not add anything new. It is just completely reowning what was there to start with but was lost. However, this process leads to the purifying of the personality, usually called the refinement of the ego.

Even the process of uncovering that we have described is experienced as a development. Seeing it as uncovering is both a theoretical formulation of the situation and a method of dealing with it. Experientially, the substance of essence is first discovered, then goes through a transformation. This transsubstantiation is the development of essence from one pure aspect to another, until the essence is completed.

Looking at it this way paves the way to arranging the aspects of essence hierarchically; the later aspects developed are higher or more refined developments. In fact, some systems view things this way.

Although it is possible to make this hierarchical arrangement, we find that experience does not correspond with it. We find that, at least to some extent, different aspects are discovered in different orders by different individuals. We also find it misleading and confusing for the student to think of essential aspects in a hierarchical order. We prefer to look at the different aspects as different parts of essence, all important and necessary, although some are more central than others. The closest analogy is the human body. All organs are necessary, and it is possible but misleading to think of them in an order. It is true that the brain is more central than the lungs, but the brain cannot function without the lungs.

From our perspective, what is discovered and realized first depends more on what sectors of the personality the individual happens to be dealing with than on an innate order of the aspects of essence. From this perspective, it is immaterial whether we look at the process as a development or an uncovering. They are equivalent formulations, provided the process is looked at experientially. Theoretically, from the perspective of an overall understanding, the process is, so far, a process of uncovering. Essence is lost, then it is retrieved.

However, seeing the process as a development applies more accurately to a certain aspect of essence, an aspect that is in a sense more central or that occupies more of a central place in the process of inner realization. Let's try to understand this.

We saw in the beginning of the chapter that work on the superego leads to the experience of space, the beginning of the experience of the void. Then the lataif are activated, and their development leads to the emergence of essence proper. The work on the superego continues because the superego has deeper roots than the castration complex, roots that originate all the way back at the beginning of life, as Edith Jacobson, for instance, has shown.[9]

However, the stage of developing essential aspects shifts the inner work on the personality from the superego more to the structure of the ego itself. We have seen, for example, that the merging essence is related psychologically to the symbiotic stage, of fundamental importance for the development of ego structure. Other aspects of essence are connected to different phases of ego development or to different sectors of its structure. Essential strength is connected, for example, to the differentiation subphase of the separation–individuation process of ego development, when the infant begins to perceive that his mother and he are two people. Joy and value are essential aspects related more to the practicing subphase of this developmental process, when the toddler is joyously exploring his capacities and environment.

The separation–individuation process leads ultimately to the development of the ego as a structure. Its final phase is that of object constancy, when the ego is formed and established as a permanent existence, separate from the environment (mother), and other people are seen to have separate existences. Finally, the ego is structured and developed, and the child permanently experiences himself as having a separate identity. The ego is seen here in a central position

---

[9] Edith Jacobson, *The Self and the Object World* (New York: International Universities Press, 1980), 19.

because everything else is really part of its structure. The ego is the product of the child's development.

Something similar happens in essential development. We should recall here that each part of the personality is an imitation of and a substitute for an aspect of essence. The ego structure as a whole is a substitute for a central aspect of essence, which has a central position similar to that of the ego.

This central aspect of essence is what we call the personal essence; in Work literature it is usually called "the pearl beyond price." Some authors, such as the Sufi Alaoddawleh Semnani, have called it the "True Ego": "The seventh and last subtle organ is related to the divine center of your being, to the eternal seal of your person (latifa haqqiya). It is the Mohammed of your being. This subtle divine center conceals the "rare Mohammedan pearl," that is to say, the subtle organ which is the True Ego."[10]

The pearl beyond price, the incomparable pearl, the personal aspect of essence is central for many important reasons. It is actually the true essential personality. It is the person. It is experienced as oneself. When the individual finally perceives it, the contented expression often is "But this is me!" The sense is of oneself as a precious being. There is then a fullness, a completeness, and a contentment. It is as if the individual feels full and complete, realized. Nothing is lacking. No more search, no desire or wanting anything else. The person feels "Now I have myself. I am a complete individual. I am full. I am fullness. I am complete. I want nothing else."

The experience of completeness and contentment is ineffable, so precious and so amazing in its effect on the mind. All agitation suddenly subsides. All preoccupation is suddenly released.

It is the experience of being oneself and not a response or reaction to something. It is not being something for somebody. It is in a sense complete freedom, the freedom to be.

Many people talk about wanting to be themselves, to have their personal freedom. But usually people are referring to their personality. Being free to be one's personality is not freedom, although it might seem so. In fact, it is the prison. But to be the pearl beyond

---

[10] Henry Corbin, *The Man of Light in Iranian Sufism* (Boulder, CO, and London: Shambhala, 1978), 125.

price is truly to be, completely and finally, free to be oneself. Now the person can experience "I am," and he is not referring to his personality.

The pearl is the real, complete, balanced, and rounded personality that psychologists believe they are talking about when they are discussing the ego. We must remember that the ego is a structure, or a structured process, whereas the pearl is essence, which means the pearl is an ontological presence. We call it the personal essence because among all the essential aspects it alone is personal. It is experienced as having a personal flavor to it, in contradistinction to impersonal. All aspects of essence, even love and kindness, are impersonal. But the pearl is personal. And this is its miraculous quality, totally unexpected and unfathomable.

Some people interested in inner development try to become objective and impersonal, to move away from identifying with the personality. The personality is personal, and so the personal feeling is mistrusted and avoided.

However, the pearl beyond price feels personal without being the personality. It has the capacity to make a personal contact with another human being and still be free, totally unconditioned, free from the past and its influences.

It is the most personally intimate aspect of oneself. Everyone recognizes what it is when he first sees it. Sometimes even the vaguest perception of it brings out the exclamation "but this feels like me, intimately me." And yet it is not selfish like the personality. The personality is based on deficiency, and this is the source of its selfishness. But the pearl is based on true value and true fullness. In fact, it is itself fullness.

All of essential development is ultimately the development of the pearl. All of the essential aspects are for the pearl, for the life, use, enjoyment, and fulfillment of the pearl. That is why in the stories it is represented as a princess of unsurpassable beauty. The joy of the essence is its joy. The love is its love. The pleasure of the essence is for it, the majesty of the essence is its grandeur, the beauty of the essence is it, itself.

The whole quest—its meaning, purpose, and completion—can be understood as the realization of the pearl beyond price. Many stories have been written about it. We include here a story from the Christian tradition:

The Hymn of the Pearl

Also known as the Hymn of the robe of Glory, or the Hymn of the Soul.

The most immediately charming of all GNOSTIC writing, perhaps dating from the early third century A.D. It begins:

> When I was a little child
>   and dwelt in the kingdom of my
>   father's house
>   and took joy in the wealth
>   and glory of my upbringing
> my parents gave me provisions
>   and sent me out
> from our homeland in the East.

They take off his glorious robes and send him down to Egypt to fetch the Pearl, which is guarded by a snake. On his arrival there, he puts on the Egyptian's clothes, but they drug him into forgetting his past and his mission. His father sends him a letter to awaken him. He charms the snake, seizes the Pearl, puts off the filthy and impure clothes he is wearing. His parents send his robe to greet him.

> Suddenly, as I looked straight at it,
>   the robe seemed like a mirror-image of
>   myself.
> I saw myself entire in it
>   In looking at it I was looking at myself.

So he returns, and does obeisance to his Father, who promises him that he shall enter with his pearl the presence of the King of Kings.[11]

Unlike other aspects of essence, this personal aspect (the pearl) goes through a process of development, growth, and expansion.

---

[11] John Ferguson, *Encyclopedia of Mysticism* (London: Thames & Hudson, 1976), 82.

Here the concepts of development and growth can be seen in their true and literal meaning. This true personality of the being is born, fed, and nourished. It grows, expands, and develops in a very specific sense. It is really the development of essence from being impersonal to being personal. Others might call it God becoming a human person, an individual. Let's try to understand this.

One way of understanding the various aspects of essence is to see them as the differentiation of the source. It is like the Gnostic story called the King of Kings. What we call the essence of the essence is the white light, and the aspects of essence are the different colors of the rainbow. The aspect of the essence of the essence, the source, and the various other aspects differentiating from it are all impersonal. When all of these differentiated aspects are realized, they are then integrated in a new synthesis, a synthesis that has a personal characteristic. This integration of all aspects of essence into a new and personal synthesis is the pearl beyond price. So from the undifferentiated source, finally there emerges a synthesis, a rounded personality that is essential.

It is interesting here to contrast this with the development of the ego. The ego is also seen by ego psychologists as the final synthesis that starts at the beginning from an undifferentiated source, what Heinz Hartmann called the undifferentiated matrix. The process of the development of the ego is seen to be really an imitation of the development of the pearl. That is why, in the Diamond Approach, instead of using the terms *ego* and *true ego*, we use the terms *pearl* and *false pearl*. In reality, the ego, indeed the personality as a whole, is nothing but the grain of sand needed for the formation and development of the pearl. In most people the grain of sand takes the place of the pearl and after a while starts thinking of itself as a precious pearl.

The process of the development of the pearl is the gradual integration of all of the aspects of essence into a new form, a new substance. When the pearl is first born, it is usually not complete; it is the essential child. It is born as a personal kernel. Then it integrates all of the aspects of essence into its very substance by spontaneous synthesis, until it is all complete, forming a harmonious human being.

Ego psychologists consider the ego to have the functions of integration and synthesis. Its synthetic function is becoming recognized as central. We see in the pearl the real and true integration. The pearl not only synthesizes; it is the synthesis itself.

This perception of the precious pearl as the complete synthesis of essential aspects is of fundamental importance. It safeguards against imbalance in inner development, for the pearl is the balance. It safeguards against prejudice and sectarianism, for it has everything in its very substance.

Some systems and teachings equilibrate themselves around the knowledge and realization of one particular essential aspect or a cluster of essential aspects. When there is no complete knowledge, it is possible through some rigorous disciplines to focus on and establish one or a few essential aspects, to the exclusion of others. This will establish a true essential presence, with the power and beauty of essence, but that presence will be incomplete and unbalanced. This limited essential development is also an effective way of avoiding having to deal with some conflict-laden sectors of the personality.

So it is obvious how differences arise between the different systems and teachings and how this can lead to prejudice and sectarianism. If only some essential aspects are developed, then some sectors of the personality are not understood, which will bring about various kinds of distortions. This is a very tricky situation to discern, especially for the individual concerned. When an individual experiences his essence, when he sees the truth, the reality, the power, and the beauty of it, it is difficult for him to realize when something is not right. The imbalance is usually explained and rationalized away by the building of a system or a teaching centered around the essential aspect or aspects known.

The systems built around awareness, for instance, will not understand and might even oppose the systems built around the merging essence. Each believes he has the truth, and both actually have the truth. But neither has the whole truth. Another clear example is the apparent contradiction between the teachings built around emptiness and the teachings built around existence.

However, if the precious pearl becomes the objective of the system, then there is an innate and built-in safeguard. To really develop and establish the pearl, all sectors of the personality have to be explored and understood. For the pearl to develop, all aspects of essence have to be freed, which will expose all sectors of the personality. Freeing it and establishing its life enables it to displace the totality of the ego structure. Then there is balance, completeness, totality, harmony, fullness, and contentment. There is then no reason to oppose someone or to convert anyone. All inner compulsion will be gone, for the person is realized, and the realization is based on fullness, richness, and value. The individual is then a mature human being, a complete person.

Some of the ancient systems downplayed the aspects and spoke only of the pearl. They discouraged preoccupation with anything along the path, including the essential aspects, short of the incomparable pearl.

In one Sufi teaching story, the seeker becomes excited when he has his first experiences of the inner world. The story refers to these experiences as the finding of some kind of delicious dessert, the *halwa* of Baghdad. Only when the seeker finds the source of the halwa does it become possible for him to see that these experiences, although wonderful, are insignificant compared to the realization of the pearl beyond price. It turns out that the halwa is nothing but the remains of the cosmetic materials that a prisoner, princess Incomparable Pearl, uses for her daily baths.[12]

The station of the pearl beyond price is so significant because it is not a matter of a state of consciousness or a state of being; it is rather the condition of the actualization of one's realization in one's life. Being becomes personal being, a complete human being living fully the life of objective truth.

IDENTITY

We have so far discussed the essential development ensuing from the work on the superego and the ego, successively. We have discussed this development in the most general and cursory fashion. We did not discuss all of the specific holes of the personality, all of the corresponding essential aspects, or all of the relationships between the aspects on the various levels of functioning. We have also omitted discussion of many other aspects of the process, other kinds

---

[12] Idries Shah, *Tales of the Dervishes* (New York, E. P. Dutton, 1970), 15–20.

of experiences and realizations, and their effect on the life of the individual. The process is very involved, rich, and powerful in its impact on the person.

We now come to the last and deepest structure of the personality, which Freud called the id. The id is the sector of the personality that is most primitive, closest to the biological roots, and that contains the instincts and their energies and drives. The instincts and their drives are still the least understood part of depth psychology. The id, however, as Freud had already pointed out, is really the basis and the ground for the whole personality.

The instincts and their drives are usually the categories that people question least. People are driven by their instincts, and this drivenness is seen as the natural course and therefore is not questioned. People are usually not interested in being free from the deep influences of their instincts. The instincts are so deep and basic and determine the personality and its life to such an extent that it does not even occur to the individual to wonder whether it is possible to be free from instinct.

The only possibility seen by depth psychology in terms of the functioning of the instincts is their repression and distortion by the developmental process. They are either functioning normally, or they are repressed and distorted. At most they can be sublimated, that is, their energies diverted into other activities. The possibility of actually surpassing the functioning of instincts is never questioned. Instincts are taken as an unalterable part of our biological existence.

Not questioning the power of the instincts is tantamount to not questioning the most tenacious sector of the personality—the sense of identity, the sense of self, or what is called in depth psychology the ego identity. In ego psychology and object relations theory, a distinction is made between ego and ego identity. The ego is the overall process and structure. But the ego identity, the self, is the organizing center, the apex of the developmental process. It is the normal sense of identity that people have. It is what the ordinary person means when he says "I." It is an identification tag designating the ego, which differentiates the individual psychologically from other people. It is responsible for the psychological boundaries of the individual. The relation of ego to ego-identity (self-concept) is explained in the following passage by Otto Kernberg, one of the foremost theorists of object relations theory:

Throughout the oedipal period and latency, the integration of the self-representations into an organized self-concept proceeds, and ego-identity, originally stemming from the integrating of good and bad self-representations at the time of object constancy is established, is further consolidated. Jacobson (1964) criticized Erikson (1956) for his excessively broad use of the term ego identity, and for his de-emphasis of infantile stages of identity formation. She nevertheless considered his concept of "identity formation" valuable, provided it included processes of organization within all structures of the psychic apparatus. She suggested that the objective process of normal identity formation is reflected in the normal subjective feeling of identity. The integration of the self-concept within the ego strongly influences the integration of superego forerunners and, in turn, superego integration strongly reinforces the integration of the ego, particularly of the self-concept.[13]

This ego identity is usually what is referred to in spiritual and Work literature as the ego. It is the ego identity that, according to most systems, has to die for essence to become master, for complete liberation. It is intimately related to self-image, because ego identity is a psychological image, or what is called in object relations theory a "representation." Object relations theory believes that the ego identity or self-representation develops gradually in the process of structuralization of the ego. The belief is that it does not exist at the beginning of life but develops through the processes of internalization and identification. But the question of where the sense of identity itself comes from never arises. Where does the mind learn that there is such a possibility of having an identity? And how does the mind know what it feels like to have one? We are not wondering here about what differentiates one identity from another; we are asking about what differentiates identity from other categories of experience. For example, what differentiates ego identity from the

---

[13] Otto Kernberg, *Internal World and External Reality* (New York, London: Jason Aronson, 1980), 99–100. Used by permission.

feeling of ego strength? Where does the sense, the feeling, the recognition of the category of identity come from?

This is a big gap in ego and self psychology that is not yet even formulated. To assume that the sense of identity develops gradually as the various self-representations coalesce does not really answer the question. What do they coalesce around, and why do they always coalesce into a very definite experiential sense, always a sense of identity? Where does the element accounting for the feeling of identity (self) come from? Also, the sense of identity is usually experientially very vague, never really isolated. The vagueness of psychoanalytical writings on this question does not mean it has to be vague; it means only that it is still vague in the minds of the authors.

This is understandable, for this sense of identity, like all other sectors of the personality, is an imitation of a certain specific aspect of essence. Ego identity is an imitation of the identity of essence, the true self. The Hindus call it the Atman.

The sense of identity of the personality exists because there is an unconscious memory of this true self. The personality's sense of identity develops through the loss of the true self. The child had it to start with, but its loss led to the development, through internalizations and identifications, of the ego sense of identity coalesced around the vague memory of the true identity. A self-representation is felt as relating to self because of this vague memory of self. This is the reason for the vagueness about identity in everybody's experience.

This true self, the spark of our life, the most alive and most brilliant aspect of essence, is, so to speak, the source of all essential aspects. It is like the star of Bethlehem, witnessing the birth of essence. Many work systems, many teachings, aim all of their efforts toward finally beholding and realizing the true self, our source, the brilliant point of it all. This true identity, this aspect of I-ness, is what Ramana Maharshi, for instance, wanted his disciples to reach when he exhorted them to contemplate the question Who am I?

To free this aspect means finally to shift the identity from the ego to the essence. This is the most difficult part of the process. Even after essence in its various aspects is uncovered and freed, the individual finds that he still believes in his personality. He still holds tenaciously to the personality. The essence is present, but the individual still thinks of himself and very often acts, if he is not paying attention, as if he is the personality. That is why the death of this identity is so strongly stressed by all true teachings. But obviously it cannot be a burning one for the individual until essence is realized because his experience is mainly limited by the personality. In fact, until then, it is very difficult for such a person to understand or appreciate the issue of the death of the personality.

For this final shift to occur, the deepest aspects of the structure of the ego identity have to be understood. Here the deep experience of ego death happens. The experience of the annihilation of the personality deepens and becomes very profound. This is because the sense of self is very much related to the functioning of instincts and in particular to survival. In fact, the whole development of the personality is primarily for survival. To understand completely the deepest truth of the ego identity is to understand the necessity of the ego and its identity for the purposes of physical survival. This is a profound question, and answering it leads to a knowledge of the relationship between essence, the personality, and the physical body.

To understand and become free from the self-concept is to become free from instincts, from biological programming and evolutionary conditioning. This is made possible by coming to understand the relationship of life and death to each other and to essence. So to live the life of essence, the life of the pearl beyond price, the identification with the personality must end, through the discovery and the realization of the true and brilliant self.

This does not mean, as some teachings have it, that the individual must experience the essential self all the time, that he must hold onto it as the most precious thing. Many systems of teaching focus on the true self, concentrate on it, identify with it, and glorify it. This will naturally bring attachment, and attachment is personality, even if it is attachment to the essential self.

What needs to happen is to free this aspect of essence for it to become a station, to become permanently available, so that it is there when its mode of operation is needed. Therefore, all of the issues around identity and selfhood must be seen and understood, including the need for or attachment to identity. The true self exposes all misunderstanding and conflicts around identity and selfhood. Resolving the issues around the essential self eliminates all identification; or rather, identification becomes a free, conscious movement.

INSTINCTS

Part of this work is to understand the instincts, to be free from unconscious biological necessity. Depth psychology formulates and recognizes two instincts: the survival instinct and the sexual instinct. We add to these two a third one: the social instinct. All three instincts involve the physical survival of the human organism. They are organized by the nervous system and the lowest three energetic centers, the first three chakras. The survival or preservation instinct is organized by the first chakra at the perineum. The sexual instinct is organized by the second chakra at the base of the spine. The social instinct is organized by the third chakra at the solar plexus. They all function for physical survival but employ different energies and different modes of experience and functioning.

We can understand instinctual functioning by observing it in the human infant. For the infant, only the survival instinct is developed and fully operative. It uses a fundamental aspect of essence for its operation, based in the first chakra. This aspect is that of strength and activity, which at the beginning of life is very closely aligned to the operation of the sympathetic branch of the autonomic nervous system (ANS). At that time this aspect of essence operates in cooperation with another fundamental aspect of essence, the merging aspect, which is closely aligned with the operation of the parasympathetic branch of the ANS.

When the infant is distressed, hungry or in pain, the strength essence floods the organism, and the sympathetic branch of the ANS is activated. This is expressed in activity—crying, thrashing, and so on. This brings the mothering person, who then by her caretaking ministrations removes the distress, by feeding or whatever. The stress is discharged, bringing about the dominance of the parasympathetic branch of the ANS, which goes along with flooding the organism with the merging essence, with its contented and quiet rest.

This cycle recurs every time there is a distress for the infant. If this distress or rising charge is not relieved, the physical survival of the organism is threatened. We see here how essence is used by the instinct of self-preservation for the regulation and maintenance of the organism. And we also see that the infant is totally dependent on its mother to complete this cycle, which is called autonomic regulation. The mother functions here, as object relations theorists say, as an auxiliary ego.

As the organism grows, the other two instincts develop concurrently with the development of the ego. The ego brings about autonomy and independence from the caretaking support of the mother. The ego then functions to provide these caretaking ministrations and to complete the cycle of autonomic regulation, independently of the mother. It is here that the other two instincts come into full operation.

Let's look at the feeding activity more closely. The child is hungry, needs food for survival, health, and growth. This brings about the arousal of the sympathetic branch of the ANS, with its increasing autonomic charge. The mother then feeds the baby, and the cycle is completed.

But the mother here did more than feed the baby. She also, by this very activity, helped the baby to discharge the rising autonomic charge of the ANS. She performed, in fact, two functions for the infant. She fed it and discharged its extra energy. The discharge of the energy, the autonomic regulation, is of great importance for the organism. Sometimes the mother just does that. It is quite well known that babies are sometimes distressed because of extra energy that they don't know how to discharge on their own. The mother, if she is attuned, functions then to facilitate the discharge of this extra and distressing buildup of energy. This regulates the economy of the autonomic nervous system, so important for the health of the nervous system and the equilibrium of the whole organism.

When the personality is developed, the ego becomes independent of the mother. The two functions of direct caretaking and autonomic regulation are then done by the ego, using the energies of the social and sexual instinct, respectively.

The sexual instinct develops to take care of the function of autonomic regulation. The charge-and-discharge cycle occurs through sexual activity, culminating in the orgastic discharge that eliminates the extra charge and tensions accumulated by the normal living of the organism. So instead of parasitic dependency on the mother, there is a mutual dependency between the two people in the couple, which performs the same function of autonomic regulation.

That sexuality functions for the elimination of extra energy and tension (autonomic regulation) has been understood and formulated by Wilhelm Reich, as in the following passage by one of his students:

> Precise clinical studies showed that in satisfactory sexual experiences this energy was somehow concentrated in the genital area and then discharged, relieving stasis in the organism. When anxiety was present no charge reached the skin and discharge could not occur. The genital could thus be looked upon as a specialized organ of the skin capable of discharging energy.
> The function of the sexual act seemed to be primarily to maintain an economic energy level in the organism.[14]

The details of how the sexual instinct, with its function of autonomic regulation, develops from the survival instincts is the topic of a future publication about sexuality and its relation to essence.

On the other hand, the caretaking activities of feeding, protection, and so on are organized by the social instinct. The ego is independent of the mother for this function but is mutually dependent on the community or society at large for the discharging of this function. Through mutual cooperation and work this need of the organism is taken care of by all individuals in the community.

So we see that the important functions of the mother are replaced, on a higher and more independent level of organization, by those of the sexual partner and society at large. And we see, although in a very general and sketchy way, how the sexual and social instincts are developments of the survival instinct.

This process of instinctual development is intimately connected to the development of the ego and its identity, as we will discuss in the book referred to above. There is a very close connection between the structure of the ego and the functions of the instincts. This means that for the personality to let go and for its identity to dissolve, the individual must deal with the issue of survival because it is underneath the functioning of all instincts. Dealing with the survival instinct will lead to understanding death and its relation to the personality and to essence.

---

[14] Elsworth F. Baker, *Man in the Trap* (New York: Farrar, Straus & Giroux, 1974), xxi.

There is an inner consistency and order for the process of essential development. There is no need for the mind to direct the process. In fact, directing the process by the mind can only lead to difficulty, for the mind does not know. Commitment to the truth is sufficient for the process to unfold. When the essential aspects are discovered and freed, when the incomparable pearl is realized, the process spontaneously unfolds in the direction of the instincts and ultimately of the survival issue.

Here it is not a matter of discovering new aspects of essence. It is a matter of letting go of the ego identity and living from the essence that is already present. In this phase of the work, everything becomes an object of study and understanding. It is no more an inner process. One's life, with all its situations, comes into focus. One's style of life—how one leads one's life in all its aspects—becomes understood and modified accordingly. The individual becomes aware of his environment and ascertains whether it supports or inhibits the life of essence. One's relationships to other people, intimate, sexual, social, and professional, all become clear and objective. Everything, every part of one's life, inner or outer, becomes conscious, no longer under the sway of the unconscious. This is a very deep and involved work. It leads to responsibility and maturity. It would be almost impossible to carry out this deep work if it were not for the presence of essence, with its penetrating power. Most of the unconscious material at this phase relates to the early months of life and even before that. It is material that is considered preverbal and, in fact, pre-personality. The mind cannot function at such depth. Only penetrating intuition and direct perception can be used effectively at such a level of work. Essence does penetrate to these deep strata of the personality. It exposes them to the light of understanding. In fact, essence is the true agent of transformation; it manifests the necessary aspects corresponding to the relevant sectors of the personality, and these aspects make possible the necessary understanding.

This knowledge needed at these very deep levels of work cannot come from outside. External knowledge is only information and is not effective at these levels where the mind does not have a structure yet. Only one's own essence can provide the necessary knowledge. Essence itself is the experiential knowledge. Also, essence is what takes the place of these abandoned sectors of the personality.

As we said above, at this stage of the work, it is not a matter of discovering new essential aspects. However, understanding the instincts and their relationship to the personality does affect essence in a particular way. All of the essential aspects, which are already realized, undergo a transformation, a development. The aspects keep their intrinsic qualities, but these qualities are taken to different dimensions. For instance, compassion remains compassion; its sense and its color stay the same. But it attains different dimensions that are needed for understanding the instincts. Compassion, like all other aspects, becomes more objective, and more universal, solid, and expanded.

Every time one of the instincts is understood, all of the aspects develop to another dimension of essence and become established there. A whole new dimension is then opened up and realized.

The incomparable pearl, the personal essence, also undergoes a transformation, and its relationship to the new dimensions becomes clear, free, and established. This process is referred to in the story above, "The Hymn of the Pearl," by the wearing of a robe.

The individual becomes even more autonomous than on the ego level. In a sense, he becomes completely autonomous. On the social level, this autonomy does not mean that he does not need society at all. It means he becomes objective about society and its functions. He no longer looks at society as if it were his mother, nor relates to it the way he did to his father or mother. He does not see it as a source of emotional support or emotional protection or nourishment. He does not look to it for admiration, approval, self-esteem, respect, position, fame, identity, and the like. The issues of friendship, trust, and power become clear. His social relations become objective, rather than clouded by the personality's assumptions and hopes about society. Society is seen for what it is, and all social interactions are seen for what they are. Society is neither rejected nor accepted but understood for what it is, what it offers, what it demands, and what it needs. Society's relation to essence and its life becomes conscious.

On the sexual level, the work is primarily to understand pleasure and to reveal all the illusions and unconsciousness about it. Not only sexual pleasure but all the kinds of pleasure, inner and outer, become understood and seen in their relation to essence and its life. This clarifies the issues of intimate relations between the sexes and their place in essential life and development. All essential aspects rise to a new dimension, where they are all seen and experienced as pleasure, as all kinds of joys and delights. The pearl reaches a new integration, and its relation to this dimension of pleasure is clarified. Both outer and inner pleasures are understood objectively and harmonized with each other and with the rest of one's life.

On the preservation or survival level, the issues encountered are those of protection, security, safety, survival, and death. The deepest sectors of the personality are encountered and understood at this point. The necessity of the personality for physical survival is comprehended and appreciated. The ego function of defense as a whole is understood and seen in its rightful place, as a substitute for some part of essence related to protection. The real protection and defense for essence and its life, the citadel of essence—what is referred to sometimes as the true conscience—is understood and realized.

An important point to understand here is that the personality does not let go easily and that this characteristic of it can be seen from a positive perspective. The personality, as we have seen consistently, contains the memory of all that was lost. To ask it to let go means, according to the unconscious, letting go of its attempt to regain all that was lost. Unconsciously, it knows what has to be there, and it is not going to clear the space completely before it is sure that everything is there. On the surface, it appears that personality wants to displace essence. This is partially true, but on the deeper levels, it was formed and developed ultimately for the protection and the survival of the organism and hence for the protection and the survival of the whole essential process. And it performs this function faithfully, even though rigidly.

Therefore, it is extremely difficult for the personality, and especially for the ego identity (self-concept), to loosen its grip and let go when it believes that only lack and emptiness will result. It knows, although vaguely and unconsciously, that richness and fulfillment are possible, and it continues to hold out for them. However, if the essential aspects are uncovered and the various functions of essence realized, it is much easier for the personality to let go.

The personality then will not be letting go out of desperation and hopelessness. It will let go because of understanding. It will melt away because it will see that its life is suffering and that the fulfillment of the life of essence is impeded by its own very existence. The personality will realize that it itself is the barrier to the life of fullness and abundance. It will see the necessity of its own death. It will long for it. And then it will not only disintegrate into emptiness, it will melt and disappear into the sweet honey of the divine essence.

Creative Discovery

The moment essence is recognized as one's being and experienced as such, a radical transformation occurs. One's life will never be the same. Although the transformation can be total, it is usually partial. Nevertheless, it is a radical transformation: the person knows for the first time what being is and that it is his true nature. As we saw at the beginning in this chapter, this discovery initiates the process of inner transformation. This transformation is both in the mind and on the essential dimension. The mind and personality are clarified steadily, and objectivity becomes more and more complete. Essence transsubstantiates into its various aspects and dimensions.

Life is no longer the exclusive domain of the personality. As essence unfolds and expands, it exposes deeper and more basic sectors of the personality, bringing about knowledge and objectivity. And these in turn allow essence to displace the personality on more and more dimensions.

The discovery of essence is the beginning of the true life. Essence, as we have seen, is not a state experienced once and then always experienced in the same way afterward. Essence is rich and endless in its aspects, qualities, dimensions, capacities, and possibilities. All of this richness starts unfolding, bringing surprise, delight, beauty, value, and fulfillment.

Life stops being the life of strife and frustration, the wish for success and the fear of failure. More than anything else, life becomes a process of creative discovery. Discovery itself becomes the heart of life. Life becomes a continual creation because essence is the creative element in us. Suffering and problems become less important, and creative discovery becomes the actual process of living.

The unfolding of essence becomes the process of living. Life is no longer a string of disconnected experiences of pleasure and pain but a flow, a stream of aliveness. One aspect manifests after another, one dimension after another, one capacity after another. There is a constant flow of understanding, insight, knowledge, and states of being.

As this unfolding proceeds, it affects the mind, the personality, and the external life. When conflicts arise, inner or outer, it is the expression of the lack of understanding of incoming essential aspects and dimensions. It is part of the creative process of living. Every new insight or knowledge is preceded by its absence. This absence is seen from the perspective of the ego as a conflict or a problem. However, if the individual is interested in the truth, the conflict is seen for what it is, an absence of a certain understanding. The presence of this understanding is the same as the presence of a certain aspect or dimension of essence, with its qualities, capacities, insights, and mode of living.

However, the center of all this understanding, insight, knowledge, discovery, creativity, conflict, and tension is the unfolding of essential presence. This flow of essential presence becomes the true experience of time instead of the linear memory time of the personality.

At the beginning, the work of understanding continues as a necessity. However, the necessity is more apparent than real. The ego believes in the necessity of its own work, but this is due to the lack of understanding of deeper essential dimensions. As these dimensions unfold and bring about their understanding, one starts seeing how the activity of the ego (the sense of self) is the main barrier, the cause of any conflict or inner suffering.

As the pearl beyond price develops and as the true self is understood and integrated, there occurs another radical transformation. The identity starts shifting from personality to essence. The individual starts experiencing himself as essence, instead of the experiencer of essence.

Experiences of ego death occur here. Inner aloneness is accepted. Personal boundaries dissolve. Essence begins to be experienced from the perspective of essence itself. One starts to understand and experience boundlessness, timelessness, not doing, innocence, and purity. Essence and mind start becoming one. This manifests either as complete absence of thoughts, or the thoughts themselves are experienced as the spontaneous outpouring of insight.

Life continues to be a process of creative discovery. The process of learning, unfolding, and expansion never stops. Essence continues to unfold, new dimensions arise, new modes of experience and insight emerge, new capacities manifest.

The process of understanding continues; however, it is not seen as a necessity, as work, but rather as the process of creative discovery itself.

Life becomes a process of creative discovery from the moment essence is recognized and experienced as one's true being. It continues to be an endless process of creative discovery when the identity shifts to essence; however, there is now the understanding that it is so. There is now the understanding and the trust that essence will bring about whatever needs to be brought about. The ego does not need to work any more. The creative process happens on its own. Ego can only obstruct it. This is true the moment essence is discovered.

Living one's life and the work on oneself become one thing: It is "His Endlessness," unfolding as a creative discovery. The shift of identity from personality to essence is nothing but the realization of the true self, the high self of essence. This experience of timelessness, spacelessness, and no-mind is also the entrance to the Beyond, to the Universal Impersonal, the Absolute that is the ground of all existence. This is the Ultimate that is beyond personality, mind, time, and even essence.

Realization then becomes more and more expressed in living, in action. Practical action becomes the action of the true being. There is efficiency, economy, simplicity, directness. One fully lives in the world but is constantly connected to the Beyond, the Supreme Reality.

EPILOGUE

THE DESIRE FOR FREEDOM, liberation, enlightenment, self-realization, inner development, or whatever it is called is not a response to a call from outside you. It is not that you hear of enlightenment, and then you want to be enlightened. It is not embarking on the journey because others, people you know, are on it. It is not a fad.

It is not a desire for self-improvement. It is not an attempt to be some kind of an ideal model you have in your mind. It is not doing something according to some beliefs and opinions you have picked up someplace, recently or in the far past.

The search is a very personal concern, an intimately personal interest in your situation. It is a response to a call deep within you. The call at the beginning is a vague, almost imperceptible and mysterious flame. It shows itself as a questioning of the disharmony you live in. It is your disharmony, as you experience it. It is your own questioning. And it is your personal yearning.

If you want to be enlightened or realized like somebody else, who you heard was able to attain, then the search is not yours yet. It is somebody else's, Buddha's or Mohammed's.

The stirring must come from you, from your depths. The questioning must be of your situation, your mind, not of some system that somebody else has set up. You can use the system to help you, but ultimately it is your life, your mind, your quest.

Enlightenment cannot be according to any system. It has to resolve and clarify your own situation. The realization must satisfy and fulfill your heart, not the standards of some system. The liberation must be of you, you personally.

The path is you, your mind and your heart. The call is your call, relevant to your life, and it speaks intimately to you.

The call, the path, and the realization are all a very intimately personal concern. Everything else is not yours, and you cannot use it for yourself or for others. But the complete resolution of your personal situation is yours, and that you can use for others too.

The quest does not bring about improvement or perfection. It brings about a maturity, a humanity, and a wisdom.

BIBLIOGRAPHY

Alexander, Franz, M.D. *Psychosomatic Medicine.* New York: W. W. Norton, 1950.

Al-Ghazzali. *The Alchemy of Happiness.* Lahore, Pakistan: Ashraf Press, 1964.

Al-Hallaj, Mansur. *The Tawasin.* Berkeley, CA, and London: Diwan Press, 1974.

Altman, Leon L., M.D. *The Dream in Psychoanalysis.* New York: International Universities Press, 1975.

Anderson, Margaret. *The Unknowable Gurdjieff.* York Beach, ME: Samuel Weiser, 1962.

'Arabi, Ibn. *Whoso Knoweth Himself.* London: Beshara Publications, 1976.

Arasteh, A. Reza. *Rumi the Persian.* Lahore, Pakistan: Ashraf Press, 1965.

Arberry, A. J. *Discourses of Rumi.* York Beach, ME: Samuel Weiser, 1977.

Assagioli, Roberto, M.D. *Psychosynthesis.* New York: Viking, 1971.

Attar, Farid ud-Din. *The Conference of the Birds.* London: Routledge & Kegan Paul, 1967; and York Beach, ME: Samuel Weiser, 1969.

Aurobindo, Sri. *Last Poems.* Pondicherry, India: Sri Aurobindo Ashram, 1952.

———. *The Life Divine.* Vol. 1 and 2. Pondicherry, India: Sri Aurobindo Ashram, 1973.

———. *The Mind of Light.* New York: E. P. Dutton, 1971.

———. *On Himself.* Pondicherry, India: Sri Aurobindo Ashram, 1973.

Avedon, John F. *An Interview with the Dalai Lama.* New York: Little-bird Publications, 1980.

Baba, Meher. *The Everything and the Nothing.* Berkeley, CA: The Beguine Library, 1971.

————. *Listen Humanity.* New York: Harper, 1971.

Baker, Elsworth F., M.D. *Man in the Trap.* New York: Macmillan, 1974.

Barker, Sarah. *The Alexander Technique.* New York: Bantam Books, 1978.

Bennet, John G. *Is There "Life" on Earth?* New York: Stonehill, 1973.

————. *The Masters of Wisdom.* London: Turnstone Books, 1977.

Berg, Charles. *Deep Analysis.* New York: W. W. Norton, 1947.

Bergson, Henri. *Duration and Simultaneity.* New York: Bobbs-Merril, 1965.

Berne, Eric, M.D. *Games People Play.* New York: Grove Press, 1967.

————. *The Structure and Dynamics of Organizations and Groups.* New York: Ballantine Books, 1975.

Bettelheim, Bruno. *The Uses of Enchantment.* New York: Vintage Books, Random House, 1977.

Bhattacharya, Deben, trans. *Songs of the Bards of Bengal.* New York: Grove Press, 1969.

Bion, W. R. *Experiences in Groups.* New York: Ballantine Books, 1974.

Blake, A. G. E. *Intelligence Now.* Ripon, England: Coombe Springs Press, 1975.

Blanck, Gertrude and Rubin. *Ego Psychology: Theory and Practice.* New York: Columbia University Press, 1979.

————. *Ego Psychology II: Psychoanalytic Developmental Psychology.* New York: Columbia University Press, 1979.

Blofeld, John. *The Importance of Living.* New York: E. P. Dutton, 1974.

————. *The Tantric Mysticism of Tibet.* New York: E. P. Dutton, 1970.

————. trans. *The Zen Teaching of Huang Po.* New York: Grove Press, 1959.

Blum, Harold P. *Psychoanalytic Explorations of Technique.* New York: International Universities Press, 1980.

Blyth, R. H. *Zen in English Literature and Oriental Classics.* New York: E. P. Dutton, 1960.

Boadella, David. *Wilhelm Reich, the Evolution of His Work.* New York: Dell, 1973.

Bowlby, John. *Attachment and Loss.* Vol. 3, *Loss.* New York: Basic Books, 1980.

Branden, Nathaniel. *The Disowned Self.* New York: Bantam Books, 1973.

Brown, J. A. C. *Techniques of Persuasion.* London: Penguin Books, 1977.

Brown, Norman O. *Love's Body.* Toronto: London House, 1966.

Brown, Spencer O. *Laws of Form.* New York: Bantam Books, Julian Press, 1972.

Castaneda, Carlos. *The Teachings of Don Juan: A Yaqui Way of Knowledge.* New York: Ballantine Books, 1968.

Cecil, Robert, com. *The King's Son.* London: Octagon Press, 1981.

Chang, Garma C. C. *The Hundred Thousand Songs of Milarepa.* New York: Harper & Row, 1970.

Conze, Edward. *Buddhism: Its Essence and Development.* New York: Harper & Row, 1959.

Corbin, Henry. *Creative Imagination in the Sufism of Ibn 'Arabi.* Princeton, NJ: Princeton University Press, 1969.

————. *The Man of Light in Iranian Sufism.* Boulder, CO: Shambhala, 1978.

————. *Spiritual Body and Celestial Earth.* Princeton, NJ: Princeton University Press, 1977.

Cox, Jan. *And Kyroot Said.* Atlanta, GA: Chan Shal Imi Press, 1980.

————. *Dialogues of Gurdjieff.* Atlanta, GA: Chan Shal Imi Society, 1976.

Dallas, Ian. *The Book of Strangers.* New York: Pantheon Books, 1972.

Daumal, Rene. *Mount Analogue.* San Francisco: City Lights Books, 1968.

————. *A Night of Serious Drinking.* Boulder: CO: Shambhala Publications, 1979.

de Hartmann, Thomas. *Our Life with Mr. Gurdjieff.* New York: Penguin Books, 1972.

Dhammasudhi, Chao Khun Sobhana. *The Real Way to Awakening.* Hertford, England: Stephen Austin and Sons, 1971.

Ed-Din, Abu Bakr Siraj. *The Book of Certainty.* York Beach, ME: Samuel Weiser, 1970.

Edward, Joyce, Nathene Ruskin, and Patsy Turrini. *Separation Individuation, Theory and Application.* New York: Basic Books, 1981.

Eliade, Mircea. *Yoga, Immortality and Freedom.* Princeton, NJ: Princeton University Press, 1973.

Evans-Wentz, W. Y., ed. *The Tibetan Book of the Dead.* New York: Oxford University Press, 1960.

_____. ed. *The Tibetan Book of the Great Liberation*. Commentary by C. G. Jung. New York: Oxford University Press, 1972.

_____. ed. *Tibetan Yoga and Secret Doctrines*. New York: Oxford University Press, 1969.

_____. ed. *Tibet's Great Yogi Milarepa*. London: Oxford University Press, 1972.

Farzan, Massud. *The Tale of the Reed Pipe*. New York: E. P. Dutton, 1974.

Fenichel, Otto, M.D. *The Psychoanalytic Theory of Neurosis*. New York: W. W. Norton, 1972.

Freud, Sigmund. *An Autobiographical Study*. New York: W. W. Norton, 1963.

_____. *The Basic Writings of Sigmund Freud*. New York: Random House, 1938.

_____. *Beyond the Pleasure Principle*. New York: W. W. Norton, 1963.

_____. *Character and Culture*. New York: Crowell-Collier, 1963.

_____. *Civilization and Its Discontents*. New York: W. W. Norton, 1962.

_____. *Collected Papers*. Vols. 1, 2, 3, 4, and 5. New York: Basic Books, 1959.

_____. *Dora, An Analysis of a Case of Hysteria*. New York: Macmillan, 1977.

_____. *The Ego and the Id*. New York: W. W. Norton, 1962.

_____. *The Future of an Illusion*. New York: W. W. Norton, 1961.

_____. *A General Introduction to Psychoanalysis*. New York: Washington Square Press, 1965.

_____. *Group Psychology and the Analysis of the Ego*. New York: W. W. Norton, 1959.

_____. *Inhibitions, Symptoms and Anxiety*. New York: W. W. Norton, 1959.

_____. *Jokes and Their Relation to the Unconscious*. New York: W. W. Norton, 1960.

_____. *Leonardo da Vinci and a Memory of His Childhood*. New York: W. W. Norton, 1964.

_____. *Moses and Monotheism*. New York: Random House, Vintage Books, 1967.

_____. *New Introductory Lectures on Psychoanalysis*. New York: W. W. Norton, 1962.

_____. *On Dreams*. New York: W. W. Norton, 1952.

————. *The Problem of Anxiety*. New York: W. W. Norton, 1965.
————. *The Psychopathology of Everyday Life*. New York: W. W. Norton, 1965.
————. *The Question of Lay Analysis*. New York: W. W. Norton, 1969.
————. *The Sexual Enlightenment of Children*. New York: Crowell-Collier, 1963.
————. *Sexuality and the Psychology of Love*. New York: Macmillan, 1974.
————. *Totem and Taboo*. New York: W. W. Norton, 1950.
Fromme, Allan. *The Ability to Love*. New York: Pocket Books, 1966.
Fromm-Reichmann, Frieda, M.D. *Principles of Intensive Psychotherapy*. Chicago: University of Chicago Press, 1950.
Gilani, Abdul Qadir. *The Revelations of the Unseen*. Lahore, Pakistan: Ashraf Press, 1972.
Goldberg, Arnold, M.D., ed. *Advances in Self Psychology*. New York: International Universities Press, 1980.
Govinda, Lama Anagarika. *Foundations of Tibetan Mysticism*. York Beach, ME: Samuel Weiser, 1971.
Groddeck, Georg. *The Book of It*. New York: Random House, Vintage Books, 1961.
Guenther, Herbert V. *The Life and Teachings of Naropa*. London: Oxford University Press, 1970.
————. *The Royal Song of Saraha*. Boulder, CO: Shambhala Publications, 1973.
————. *The Tantric View of Life*. Boulder, CO: Shambhala Publications, 1972.
Gurdjieff, G. I. *Beelzebub's Tales to his Grandson, 2nd Book*. New York: E. P. Dutton, 1973.
————. *Beelzebub's Tales to his Grandson, 3rd Book*. New York: E. P. Dutton, 1973.
————. *Meetings with Remarkable Men*. New York: E. P. Dutton, 1963.
————. *Views from the Real World*. New York: E. P. Dutton, 1973.
Gyatsho, His Holiness Tenzin, The XIVth Dalai Lama of Tibet. *The Opening of the Wisdom Eye*. Wheaton, IL: Theosophical Publishing House, 1981.
Haley, Jay. *Problem Solving Therapy*. San Francisco, Washington, London: Jossey-Bass, 1977.
————. *Uncommon Therapy*. New York: W. W. Norton, 1973.
Hammarskjold, Dag. *Markings*. New York: Alfred A. Knopf, 1964.

Hartmann, Heinz. *Ego Psychology and the Problem of Adaptation*. New York: International Universities Press, 1945.

Herrigel, Eugen. *Zen*. New York: McGraw-Hill, 1964.

Higgins, Mary, and Chester Raphael, M.D. *Reich Speaks of Freud*. Rexdale, Ontario: Ambassador Books, 1967.

Hoffman, Bob. *Getting Divorced from Mother and Dad*. New York: E. P. Dutton, 1976.

Horner, Althea J. *Object Relations and the Developing Ego in Therapy*. New York and London: Jason Aronson, 1979.

Horney, Karen, M.D. *The Neurotic Personality of Our Time*. New York: W. W. Norton, 1964.

————. *New Ways in Psychoanalysis*. New York: W. W. Norton, 1939.

————. *Our Inner Conflicts*. New York: W. W. Norton, 1966.

————. *Self-Analysis*. New York: W. W. Norton, 1942.

Humphreys, Christmas. *Zen Buddhism*. New York: Macmillan, 1949.

Isherwood, Christopher. *Ramakrishna and His Disciples*. New York: Simon and Schuster, 1970.

Jacobson, Edith, M.D. *The Self and the Object World*. New York: International Universities Press, 1980.

James, William. *The Varieties of Religious Experience*. New York: New American Library, 1964.

Jones, Ernest. *The Life and Work of Sigmund Freud*. New York: Basic Books, 1961.

Jones, Franklin (Bubba Free John). *The Knee of Listening*. San Raphael, CA: Dawn Horse Press, 1973.

Joshi, Vasant. *The Awakened One: The Life and Work of Bhagwan Shree Rajneesh*. New York: Harper and Row, 1982.

Jung, Carl G. *Man and His Symbols*. New York: Dell, 1969.

————. *Psyche and Symbol*. Edited by Violet S. de Laszlo. New York: Doubleday Anchor Books, 1958.

————. *Psychological Reflections*. Edited by Jolande Jacobi. New York: Harper and Row, 1961.

Kernberg, Otto, M.D. *Borderline Conditions and Pathological Narcissism*. New York: Jason Aronson, 1983.

————. *Internal World and External Reality*. New York: Jason Aronson, 1980.

————. *Object Relations Theory and Clinical Psychoanalysis*. New York: Jason Aronson, 1979.

Khan, Hazrat Inayat. *The Mind-World*. Geneva: The Sufi International Headquarters Publishing Society, 1955.

Khayaam, Omar. *Rubaiyyat*. Translated by Robert Graves and Omar Ali Shah. Tucson, AZ: Omen Press, 1972.

——————. *The Rubaiyat.* New York: Peter Pauper Press.

Kohut, Heinz. *The Restoration of the Self.* New York: International Universities Press, 1981.

Korzybski, Alfred. *Science and Sanity.* Lakeville, CT: The International Non-Aristotelian Library, 1958.

Krishna, Gopi. *Kundalini, the Evolutionary Energy in Man.* Boulder, CO: Shambhala Publications, 1976.

Krishnamurti, J. *Commentaries on Living.* 2d ser. Wheaton, IL:The Theosophical Publishing House, 1981.

——————. *Commentaries on Living.* 3d ser. Wheaton, IL: The Theosophical Publishing House, 1977.

——————. *The Flight of the Eagle.* New York: Harper and Row, 1971.

——————. *Freedom from the Known.* London: Victor Gollancz, 1969.

——————. *Krishnamurti's Journal.* New York: Harper and Row, 1982.

Kudian, Mischa. *Three Apples Fell from Heaven.* London: Rupert Hart-Davis, 1969.

Laing, R. D. *The Divided Self.* London: Penguin Books, 1965.

——————. *Do You Love Me?* New York: Ballantine Books, 1976.

——————. *Knots.* New York: Random House, Vintage Books, 1972.

——————. *Sanity, Madness and the Family.* London: Penguin Books, 1977.

——————. *The Politics of Experience.* New York: Pantheon Books, 1967.

——————. *The Politics of the Family and Other Essays.* New York: Vintage Books, Random House, 1972.

Lal, P. *The Dhammapada.* New York: Farrar, Straus and Giroux, 1972.

Langs, Robert, M.D. *The Bipersonal Field.* New York: Jason Aronson, 1976.

Lauf, Detlef Ingo. *Secret Doctrines of the Tibetan Book of the Dead.* Boulder, CO: Shambhala Publications, 1977.

Lax, Ruth F., Sheldon Bach, and J. Alexis Burland. *Rapprochement: The Critical Subphase of Separation–Individuation.* New York and London: Jason Aronson, 1980.

Leadbeater, C. W. *The Chakras.* Wheaton, IL: The Theosophical Publishing House, 1969.

Lefort, Rafael. *The Teachers of Gurdjieff.* York Beach, ME: Samuel Weiser, 1971.

Lings, Martin. *What Is Sufism?* Berkeley, CA: University of California Press, 1977.

Lowen, Alexander, M.D. *The Betrayal of the Body.* London: Collier Books, 1969.

————. *Depression and the Body.* New York: Coward-McCann and Geoghegan, 1972.

————. *Love and Orgasm.* New York: New American Library, 1965.

————. *Pleasure.* New York: Coward-McCann and Geoghegan, 1970.

Luce, Gay Gaer. *Body Time.* New York: Pantheon Books, 1971.

Luk, Charles (Lu K'uan Yu). *Taoist Yoga: Alchemy and Immortality.* York Beach, ME: Samuel Weiser, 1970.

Lutyens, Mary. *Krishnamurti: The Years of Awakening.* New York: Avon Books, 1976.

————. *Krishnamurti: The Years of Fulfillment.* New York: Farrar, Straus, and Giroux, 1983.

Mahler, Margaret, Fred Pine, and Anni Bergman. *The Psychological Birth of the Human Infant.* New York: Basic Books, 1975.

Mann, W. Edward. *Orgone, Reich and Eros.* New York: Simon and Schuster, 1973.

Marcuse, Herbert. *One Dimensional Man.* Boston: Beacon Press, 1966.

Masterson, James F., M.D. *The Narcissistic and Borderline Disorders.* New York: Brunner/Mazel, 1981.

Merton, Thomas. *Mystics and Zen Masters.* New York: Dell, 1967.

————. *Zen and the Birds of Appetite.* New York: New Directions, 1968.

Miller, Alice. *Prisoners of Childhood.* New York: Basic Books, 1981.

Muktananda, Swami. *American Tour 1970.* Piedmond, CA: Shree Gurudev Siddha Yoga Ashram, 1974.

————. *Guru.* New York: Harper and Row, 1971.

Muses, Charles, and Arthur M. Young. *Consciousness and Reality.* New York: Outerbridge and Lazard, 1972.

Nafzawi, Shaykh. *The Perfumed Garden.* Translated by Sir Richard Burton. New York: G. P. Putnam's Sons, 1964.

Nagarjuna and Lama Mipham. *Golden Zephyr.* Translated by Leslie Kwamura. Emeryville, CA: Dharma Press, 1975.

Naranjo, Claudio, M.D. *The Healing Journey.* New York: Pantheon Books, 1973.

————. *On the Psychology of Meditation.* New York: Viking, 1971.

————. *The One Quest.* New York: Viking, 1972.

————. *The Techniques of Gestalt Therapy.* Berkeley, CA: Sat Press, 1973.

Neumann, Erich. *Amor and Psyche.* Princeton, NJ: Princeton University Press, 1971.

_____. *The Origins and History of Consciousness.* Princeton, NJ: Princeton University Press, 1973.

Nasr, Seyyed Hussein. *Sufi Essays.* New York: Schocken Books, 1977.

Nicoll, Maurice. *Psychological Commentaries on the Teaching of Gurdjieff and Ouspensky,* Vols. 1–5. London: Stuart and Watkins, 1970.

Nott, C. S. *Teachings of Gurdjieff.* York Beach, ME: Samuel Weiser, 1971.

Nurbakhsh, Dr. Javad. *What the Sufis Say.* London: Khaniqahi-Nimatullahi Publications, 1980.

Ogden, Thomas H., M.D. *Projective Identification and Psychotherapeutic Technique.* New York and London: Jason Aronson, 1982.

Ornstein, Robert E. *On the Experience of Time.* London: Penguin Books, 1969.

Osborne, Arthur, trans. *The Collected Works of Ramana Maharshi.* York Beach, ME: Samuel Weiser, 1969.

Ouspensky, P. D. *The Fourth Way.* New York: Random House, Vintage Books, 1971.

_____. *In Search of the Miraculous.* New York: Harcourt, Brace and World, 1949.

_____. *The Psychology of Man's Possible Evolution.* New York: Random House, Vintage Books, 1974.

_____. *The Strange Life of Ivan Osokin.* New York: Penguin Books, 1971.

_____. *Talks with a Devil.* New York: Alfred A. Knopf, 1973.

Paolino, Thomas J., Jr., M.D. *Psychoanalytic Psychotherapy.* New York: Brunner/Mazel, 1981.

Paul, I. H. *The Form and Technique of Psychotherapy.* Chicago: University of Chicago Press, 1978.

Perls, Fritz S., M.D. *Ego, Hunger and Aggression.* New York: Vintage Books, 1969.

_____. *The Gestalt Approach and Eye Witness to Therapy.* Ben Lomond, CA: Science and Behavior Books, 1973.

_____. *In and Out of the Garbage Pail.* Moab, UT: Real People Press, 1969.

Plato. *The Last Days of Socrates.* Translated by Hugh Trenennick. New York: Penguin Books, 1977.

_____. *Meno.* Translated by Benjamin Jowett. Indianapolis: Bobbs-Merrill, 1976.

_____. *Protagoras.* Translated by Benjamin Jowett. Indianapolis: Bobbs-Merril, 1956.

————. *The Republic of Plato*. Translated by Francis MacDonald Cornford. London: Oxford University Press, 1941.

Prabhavananda, Swami, trans. *Bhagavad-Gita*. New York: New American Library, 1951.

Progoff, Ira. *The Death and Rebirth of Psychology*. New York: McGraw-Hill, 1973.

Rajneesh, Bhagwan Shree. *The Book of the Secrets*. New York: Harper and Row, 1977.

————. *The Guest: Talks on Kabir*. Poona, India: Ma Yoga Laxmi Rajneesh Foundation, 1981.

————. *Meditation: The Art of Ecstasy*. New York: Harper and Row, 1976.

————. *Only One Sky*. New York: E. P. Dutton, 1975.

————. *The Psychology of the Esoteric*. New York: Harper and Row, 1979.

Reich, Wilhelm. *The Cancer Biopathy*. Translated by Andrew White with Mary Higgins and Chester M. Raphael, M.D. New York: Farrar, Straus and Giroux, 1973.

————. *Character Analysis*. Translated by Vincent R. Carfagno. New York: Simon and Schuster, 1972.

————. *Ether, God and Devil*. Translated by Therese Pol. New York: Farrar, Straus and Giroux, 1973.

————. *The Function of the Orgasm*. Translated by Vincent R. Carfagno. New York: Simon and Schuster, 1975.

————. *Genitality*. Translated by Philip Schmitz. New York: Farrar, Straus and Giroux, 1980.

————. *The Impulsive Character and Other Writings*. Translated by Barbara G. Koopman. New York: New American Library, 1974.

————. *The Mass Psychology of Fascism*. Translated by Vincent R. Carfagno. New York: Farrar, Straus and Giroux, 1970.

————. *People in Trouble*, Vol. 2. Translated by Philip Schmitz. New York: Farrar, Straus and Giroux, 1976.

————. *Selected Writings*. New York: Farrar, Straus and Giroux, 1960.

Reik, Theodore. *Listening with the Third Ear*. New York: Grove Press, 1948.

Reps, Paul, com., *Zen Flesh, Zen Bones*. New York: Doubleday, 1956.

Roberts, Jane. *Seth Speaks*. New York: Bantam Books, 1972.

Rumi, Jalal al-Din. *Mystical Poems of Rumi*. Translated by A. J. Arberry. Chicago: University of Chicago Press, 1968.

Sana'i, Hakim Abu' L-Majd Majdud. *The Enclosed Garden of the Truth.* Edited and translated by Major J. Stephenson. York Beach, ME: Samuel Weiser, 1968.

Sandweiss, Samuel H., M.D. *Sai Baba. . . The Holy Man and the Psychiatrist.* San Diego, CA: Birth Day Publishing Company, 1976.

Satprem. *Sri Aurobindo, or the Adventure of Consciousness.* Pondicherry, India: Sri Aurobindo Ashram Press, 1973.

Sayadaw, Mahasi. *The Satipatthana Vipassana Meditation.* Elgin, AZ: Unity Press, no date.

Shabistari, Mahmud. *The Secret Garden.* London: Octagon Press, 1969.

Shah, Idries. *Caravan of Dreams.* New York: Penguin Books, 1972.

_____. *The Dermis Probe.* New York: E. P. Dutton, 1971.

_____. *The Exploits of the Incomparable Mulla Nasrudin.* New York: E. P. Dutton, 1971.

_____. *The Hundred Tales of Wisdom.* London: Octagon Press, 1978.

_____. *Learning How to Learn.* London: Octagon Press, 1978.

_____. *The Magic Monastery.* New York: E. P. Dutton, 1972.

_____. *Neglected Aspects of Sufi Study.* London: Octagon Press, 1977.

_____. *Oriental Magic.* New York: E. P. Dutton, 1973.

_____. *A Perfumed Scorpion.* London: Octagon Press, 1978.

_____. *The Pleasantries of the Incredible Mulla Nasrudin.* New York: E. P. Dutton, 1971.

_____. *Reflections.* New York: Penguin Books, 1972.

_____. *Seeker after Truth.* London: Octagon Press, 1982.

_____. *The Subtleties of the Inimitable Mulla.* New York: E. P. Dutton, 1973.

_____. *The Sufis.* New York: Doubleday, 1964.

_____. *Tales of the Dervishes.* New York: E. P. Dutton, 1970.

_____. *Thinkers of the East.* London: Jonathan Cape, 1971.

_____. *A Veiled Gazelle.* London: Octagon Press, 1977.

_____. *The Way of the Sufi.* New York: E. P. Dutton, 1970.

_____. *Wisdom of the Idiots.* New York: E. P. Dutton, 1971.

Shah, Ikbal Ali. *The Spirit of the East.* London: Octagon Press, 1973.

Shamsu-'d-din Ahmed, El Eflaki. *Legends of the Sufis.* London: The Theosophical Publishing House, 1976.

Shapiro, David. *Neurotic Styles.* New York: Basic Books, 1965.

Sharpe, Ella Freeman. *Collected Papers on Psychoanalysis.* New York: Brunner/Mazel, 1978.

_____. *Dream Analysis.* New York: Brunner/Mazel, 1978.

Shattock, E. H. *An Experiment in Mindfulness*. York Beach, ME: Samuel Weiser, 1970.

Smith, Huston. *The Religions of Man*. New York: Harper and Row, 1958.

Speeth, Kathleen Riordan. *The Gurdjieff Work*. Berkeley, CA: And/Or Press, 1976.

Stanislavski, Constantin. *Building a Character*. New York: Theater Arts Books, 1977.

Suzuki, D.T. *An Introduction to Zen Buddhism*. New York: Grove Press, 1957.

————. *What Is Zen?* New York: Harper and Row, 1972.

————. *Zen Buddhism*. New York: Doubleday, 1956.

Suzuki, Shunryu. *Zen Mind, Beginner's Mind*. New York and Tokyo: Walker/Weatherhill, 1971.

Tabriz, Divani Shamsi. *Rumi*. Berkeley, CA, and London: Diwan Press, 1974.

Tagore, Rabindranath. *The Religion of Man*. Boston: Beacon Press, 1966.

Teilhard de Chardin, Pierre. *Hymn of the Universe*. New York: Harper and Row, 1972.

Thomas, Lewis. *The Lives of a Cell*. New York: Bantam Books, 1974.

Trungpa, Chogyam. *Born in Tibet*. New York: Penguin Books, 1971.

————. *Cutting Through Spiritual Materialism*. Boulder, CO: Shambhala Publications, 1973.

————. *Journey Without Goal*. Boulder, CO, and London: Prajna Press, 1981.

————. *Meditation in Action*. Boulder, CO: Shambhala Publications, 1970.

————. *Mudra*. Boulder, CO: Shambhala Publications, 1972.

Trungpa, Chogyam and Herbert V. Guenther. *The Dawn of Tantra*. Boulder, CO: Shambhala Publications, 1975.

Tulku, Tarthang. *Hidden Mind of Freedom*. Berkeley, CA: Dharma Press, 1981.

————. *Time, Space and Knowledge*. Berkeley, CA: Dharma Press, 1977.

Tzu, Lao. *Tao Te Ching*. Translated by D. C. Lau. New York: Penguin Books, 1968.

Waelder, Robert. *Basic Theory of Psychoanalysis*. New York: Schocken Books, 1964.

Waters, Frank. *Book of the Hopi*. New York: Ballantine Books, 1969.

Watts, Alan. *The Book.* New York: Random House, 1966.

Whinfield, E. H. *The Teachings of Rumi.* New York: E. P. Dutton, 1975.

Winnicott, D.W. *The Maturational Process and the Facilitating Environment.* New York: International Universities Press, 1980.

Wong Mou-Lam, trans. *The Sutra of Hui Neng.* London: The Buddhist Society, 1966.

Wycoff, James. *Wilhelm Reich: Life Force Explorer.* Greenwich, CT: Fawcett Publications, 1973.

Yutang, Lin. *The Importance of Living.* New York: Reynal and Hitchcock, 1938.

Zimmer, Heinrich. *The King and the Corpse.* Edited by Joseph Campbell. Princeton, NJ: Princeton University Press, 1973.

RIDHWAN

*A Work School dedicated to the discovery,
development, and preservation of the Human Essence.*

The source of our Work is the same as that of all genuine Schools of the Work of any time or place. In our School, however, we do the work of liberation using a new method. In this method we have integrated in a specific and precise way some of the ancient knowledge about the Human Essence and its development with the contemporary body of knowledge that shapes the present day mentality. In particular, we have studied, expanded, and fitted various aspects of knowledge and techniques from the major schools of psychology and psychotherapy, including the body approaches, to the work of liberation and realization. Our methods and techniques have, in effect, developed in the present environment, amidst the latest findings of the various psychological schools.

For more information, write:

Ridhwan
P.O. Box 10114   or
Berkeley, CA 94709

Ridhwan School
P.O. Box 17491
Boulder, CO 80308